THE WORLD OF
ARTHUR RANSOME

Christina Hardyment

THE WORLD OF ARTHUR RANSOME

FRANCES LINCOLN LIMITED

PUBLISHERS

To Paul and Cecilia Flint,
who make me feel at home in
Ransome country

Frances Lincoln Limited
www.franceslincoln.com

The World of Arthur Ransome
Copyright © Frances Lincoln Limited 2012
Text copyright © Christina Hardyment 2012
Illustrations copyright as listed on page 160
First Frances Lincoln edition 2012

A catalogue record for this book is available
from the British Library.

978-0-7112-3297-6

Printed and bound in China
9 8 7 6 5 4 3 2 1

RIGHT Paul and Caroline Johnson's
Arbeia in Peel Island's 'secret harbour'
PAGE 1 Ransome's cartoon of himself
relaxing by the fireside, with a pipe, and,
on the mantlepiece, a bottle of rum and
a jar of tobacco (no date)
PAGE 2 Friar's Crag, Derwent Water,
inspired the setting of the 'Peak in
Darien', the opening scene of *Swallows
and Amazons*
PAGE 3 Ransome's sign-off sketch
of himself
OPPOSITE From Arthur
Ransome's *Book of Friendship*

CONTENTS

PREFACE

'Houses are but badly-built boats so firmly aground that you cannot think of moving them . . . The desire to build a house is the tired wish of a man content thenceforward with a single anchorage. The desire to build a boat is the desire of youth, unwilling yet to accept the idea of a final resting-place.'

Arthur Ransome, Racundra's First Cruise

Arthur Ransome moved countless times, and late in life accurately referred to his succession of London dwellings as camps. And yet, both in his books and in his behaviour, he reveals a deep interest in matters domestic. Whether in a London bedsit, a fellside tent or a cabin on the Baltic or the Broads, he had the nomad's knack of making himself comfortable, and displayed ingenuity and imagination whether he was boiling haddock in a kettle, contriving bookshelves out of packing cases, making marmalade while at sea, frying trout over a lakeside campfire or sending a shopping list by hoisting geometric shapes. All his life, he loved indoor games. A brilliant chess player, he also enjoyed card-games, darts and billiards.

However, one enduring place is inseparably associated with him: the amalgam of Windermere's water and Coniston's hinterland that he immortalized as the Lake in the North. He came to Coniston Water before he could walk or talk; he spent his old age in a remote little house between the two lakes. During the eighty-three years between his first holiday at Nibthwaite in 1884 and his burial in Rusland in 1967, he never forgot that heartland. 'No matter where I was, wandering about the world, I used at night to look for the North Star and, in my mind's eye, could see the beloved skyline of

Ransome's portrait by John Thomas Gilroy hangs in his beloved Garrick Club

great hills beneath it.' He returned there again and again, lodging in and owning a succession of attractive houses and never failing to go down to the lakeshore to dip his fingers in the water 'as a proof to myself that I had indeed come home'.

Boats were the other love of his life. The 'desire of youth' to build a boat had not abated even when he was sixty-eight, and in poor health. Of the six he owned, five survive; only *Racundra* is no more. *Nancy Blackett*, the 'best little ship' he ever owned, and which he made famous as *Goblin* in *We Didn't Mean to Go To Sea*, now belongs to the Nancy Blackett Trust. A star of many boat shows, she is accessible to all. You can even sail to Holland in her yourself.

The three major books about Ransome's life have all been dominated by the eleven years he spent in Eastern Europe. This one corrects that imbalance by concentrating on what lovers of his books are most interested in: the story behind the stories. It tells of his discovery of the Lake in the North, of how he learnt to sail first in the sturdy lug-sailed dinghy *Swallow* and then in the Baltic, and of the deep love of family – both his own and the one that he wholeheartedly adopted – that made him want to write for children. It explains how he came to write *Swallows and Amazons* and the eleven books that followed it, and shows how every one of the twelve books was a tribute to the people and places he loved.

THE MAKING OF AN AUTHOR
(1884–1912)

INHERITANCE

'I began life with a vast number of uncles and aunts.'
Arthur Ransome, Autobiography

Arthur Ransome was proud of his family. Whenever he moved house, portraits and photographs of both ancestors and living relatives, and pictures of the places in which they lived, moved with him. When sailing on the Norfolk Broads and cruising the east coast rivers, he was fond of telling friends that the first recorded Ransomes were seventeenth-century East Anglian millers and Quakers. Later they became Norwich bankers and Ipswich iron founders.

He inherited his lifelong love of the Lakes from the northern branch of the family founded when John Atkinson Ransome (1779–1837) moved to Manchester, where he practised as a surgeon. Among his eight children was Tom Ransome (1825–97), Arthur Ransome's grandfather. Arthur remembered him as 'a first-rate field naturalist, as interesting a companion on a country walk as any small boy could wish, and a very good, ingenious fisherman'. Tom married his childhood sweetheart, Hannah Jackson, and became a retail chemist in Manchester. In 1851, their first child Cyril, who would become Arthur's father,

Arthur's father, Cyril Ransome

was born. In 1856 Tom brought his family north, to grow up in the healthy seaside air of his uncle's house at Hest Bank, on the shores of Morecambe Bay. By 1864 he and Hannah had six children. Hannah died in 1866, and within two years Tom had married the children's governess, Annie Shepherd. By 1881, he had six more children.

As a boy, Cyril found his father excellent company. When he became a weekly boarder at Lancaster's Royal Grammar School, Tom used to accompany him every Monday and Friday on the 3-mile walk along the canal between Hest Bank and Lancaster, commenting on its flora, fauna and likely fishing spots. Tom's favourite fishing river, the Bela, would be loved by Cyril all his life, and later by Arthur. But Cyril's early affinity with his father faded. He resented Tom's second marriage, and the long stream of step-siblings. He took to spending holidays with his uncle, John Ransome, vicar of Lindale-in-Cartmel, who was married to Emily Binyon, aunt of the poet Laurence, later a good friend to Arthur. These holidays established Cyril's lifelong love for the southern Lakes and their rivers. Family matters were made worse because although Tom was an ingenious inventor of both fishing and photographic notions, he had no business sense, and neither his chemical firm nor his inventions earned enough money to maintain his huge family. Ever optimistic, he gambled on the stock market. He lost more often than he won, and over the next few decades became steadily more indebted to relatives.

Some of Tom's debts were incurred ensuring that his eldest son received a first-class education. Cyril spent six years at Oxford and dreamt of a career in politics, but when he discovered the extent of his father's debts, he dutifully set himself to pay them off by taking up the much more reliable career of teaching. Many of Cyril's closest friends taught at Rugby, the school made legendary by Thomas Arnold. After a brief spell at the Oxford Military College, Cyril followed them there, but by 1879, he was Professor of Modern Literature and History at the Yorkshire College (later Leeds University). Soon he was rattling off history textbooks so successful that by the end of his life he had not only paid off Tom Ransome's debts but provided a long-lasting source of income for his own family.

In 1882, Cyril, now thirty-one, married twenty-year-old Edith Boulton, daughter of the eminent artist of the Australian landscape Edward Boulton, and they moved to 6 Ash Grove, a modest mid-Victorian terraced house in the north Leeds suburb of Headingley. Edith, who was working as a governess when she met Cyril, was intelligent and serious-minded, and had inherited her father's artistic talent. It was a marriage of equals, which influenced their son Arthur's ever-generous attitude to women. 'I like you to be independent and think for yourself,' Cyril wrote in a courtship letter. 'I know among weak and conventional people it is assumed that wives think just like their husbands and it is thought so nice and pretty, while I think it is simply degrading to one and demoralizing to the other.' As well as being a talented painter, Edith was an able writer, and helped Cyril with his work.

Edith and Cyril's first child, Arthur Michell Ransome, was born in 1884. His names reflect his godfathers, both Oxford

Arthur's mother, Edith Ransome

Snowdonia, by Edward Baker Boulton, Edith's father

contemporaries of Cyril: Arthur Acland, with whom he wrote textbooks, and W. C. Michell, a housemaster at Rugby. Cecily was born a year later, Geoffrey in 1887 and Joyce, the youngest, in 1892. Arthur's autobiography records how stimulating their childhood was: introduced early to languages (a French nurse, Latin lessons from Cyril); provided with the best of children's books, a toy theatre, unlimited pets, carefully chosen tutors and much roaming out-of-doors, both on the moors that edge the north of Leeds and during holidays. The family moved to larger and better houses, finally settling in 1894 at St Chad's Villas in the Otley Road, Headingley. The house is now the Ascot Grange Hotel.

Throughout his early life, Ransome was surrounded by interesting relations. His mother's charismatic father, Edward

Boulton, visited from Australia with exotic tales of bushwackers and boomerangs, and her redoubtable mother, Emma, taught him to play chess. His father's spirited aunt Susan Ransome lived in Windermere, and Arthur, often desperately homesick while at prep school there, found her prettily gothic terraced house above the railway station a miraculous respite from uncongenial lessons and team games. Both these were made the more miserable because nobody spotted that he was extremely short-sighted. He had Sunday dinner with Aunt Susan every week, and sometimes accompanied her on scrambles across the fells after the fox hunt, and to archery contests on Belle Isle.

An early photograph of Arthur shows an ebullient little boy, with a mischievous air. Although Cyril often had to come the stern father, he must secretly have been hugely amused by his

LEFT Arthur (centre) with Eric
Eddison and their tutor, Mr Pegg

OPPOSITE
ABOVE In this letter sent to his mother
from prep school, Arthur pleads for
mice and a cage
BELOW Arthur wrote 'The Desert
Island' when he was six

son's exploits. At the age of four, Arthur earned his first book, *Robinson Crusoe*, by showing his disbelieving father that he could read it. At the age of six he wrote one of his own, 'The Desert Island', closely modelled on R. M. Ballantyne's *The Coral Island*. Being the oldest of his siblings made him ringmaster of their adventures. They were inspired in part by the books they read, in part by the long summer holidays the family took on the shores of Coniston Water, deep in Westmorland.

NIBTHWAITE

*'Always that country has been "home", and smoky old Leeds,
though well-beloved, was never as real as Swainson's farm.'*
Arthur Ransome, Autobiography

During term, Arthur saw little of his father, who lectured five days a week, fished and shot every weekend, and spent the evenings with his working men's club, his Conversation Club and his textbooks, besides finding time for political canvassing. But in the long summer vacation, Cyril came into his own. Keen to instil his love for the Lake Country into his family, he took them there as often as he could, beginning in September 1884, nine months after Arthur was born. That year, Cyril records in a memoir, 'We began to go to Mr John Swainson's, Nibthwaite, a farmhouse at the foot of Coniston where we spent some of our happiest hours, and the children enjoyed the early taste of country life.' Memories of those weeks became imprinted on Arthur's mind:

> Tea was always ready for our arrival . . . Then we were free in paradise, sniffing remembered smells as we ran about making sure that familiar things were still in their places. I used first of all to race down to the lake, to the old stone harbour . . . where the Swainsons' boat, our boat, was pulled up halfway out of the shallow, clear water which always seemed alive with minnows. I had a private rite to perform. Without letting the others know what I was doing, I had to dip my hand in the water, as a greeting to the beloved lake or as a proof to myself that I had indeed come home.

Having observed the state of the river as they wound up the Crake Valley, Cyril usually disappeared with a rod on arrival, leaving Edith, the nurse and Annie Swainson to unpack – no mean task. The family's luggage included quantities of fishing kit, bedding, clothes for all weathers, Edith's painting materials, transfers to amuse the children on rainy days and a large tin bath. Water came from the beck, and was heated on a coal-fired kitchen range. These were days of candles, oil lights and outside loos. Swainson's earth closet had two large holes in its capacious wooden seat, but not for sociability. Each had a deepish pit underneath it, and after each use, a shovelful of ash and earth was thrown in. When the first was filled, which took several months, its lid was closed and the contents left to break down into excellent fertilizer, while the other was used. In between was a much smaller hole, into which the men peed to provide urine. This was used to remove stains from clothes.

After checking that nothing in the house had been changed, Arthur would inspect the cowsheds, the beehives and the damson orchard, and crawl under the bridge over the beck, just as Titty and Roger do in *Swallowdale*. The damsons and the bridge over the beck are still there; so too is the Knickerbockerbreaker, 'a smooth precipitous rock easy to climb from one side for the pleasure of sliding down its face to the damage of my knickerbockers which, when they were threadbare, kind Annie Swainson would darn *in situ*'.

The children petted the farm animals, helped with haymaking and butter-churning, picked mushrooms and blackberries. When fishing and book-writing allowed, Cyril took them for walks; like his father, he was a first-rate naturalist. Charcoal-burners

RIGHT Nibthwaite, at the
southern end of Coniston Water,
showing Laurel House on the left,
and 'Octopus Lagoon' in the
River Crake
BELOW Charcoal-burners on
the shores of Coniston Water,
1908, watercolour by Alfred
Heaton Cooper

had pitsteads and wigwams in the lakeside woods; they appear in both *Swallows and Amazons* and *Swallowdale*. Arthur watched eels writhing in the eel coop in the pool below the old bobbin mill on the Crake at Spark Bridge, and met local characters who feature in his stories. Cyril took the older children as beaters on his shooting expeditions, and gave them coloured floats to watch as they fished for perch. He got Arthur to row him along the shore of the lake, following the family spaniel Carla as she splashed in the shallows to drive out pike.

High behind Nibthwaite is an outcrop of rocks with a commanding view up the lake; the children's imagination converted it into a boat. They called it *Gondola* after the sleek black-hulled passenger steamer that called at various quays along the lakeshore in the summertime. Its gilded serpent figurehead

LEFT *Gondola* as she looked in Arthur's childhood
BELOW 1930 postcard of *Gondola*, marked up by Ransome as a guide to illustrators of *Swallows and Amazons*

RIGHT *Gondola* today, restored to her full glory

708 THE "GONDOLA" ON CONISTON LAKE
(ABRAHAMS' SERIES)

Houseboat something like this

THE WORLD OF ARTHUR RANSOME

was an Italianate touch intended to please Coniston's mage, the great John Ruskin, who lived halfway along the east side of Coniston Water at Brantwood. As a small boy, Arthur was occasionally allowed to steer *Gondola*, with friendly old Captain Hamill close behind him. Thirty-five years later, when he was marking up Lakeland postcards as guides for Clifford Webb, who had been commissioned to provide illustrations for *Swallows and Amazons*, Arthur gave him one of *Gondola* in her early glory. 'Houseboat something like this' he wrote on it, adding Captain Flint's elephant flag and a stern canopy. After the decline of steam in the face of the diesel engine, *Gondola* was decommissioned, and did indeed become a houseboat on Coniston after going out of service in 1938. By the early 1970s, she was little more than a wreck, but a group of National Trust enthusiasts raised enough money to restore her, and now she is once again the most glorious craft on the lake: a piece of living Ransome history.

The Ransomes' holidays were sociable affairs. Cyril had a wealthy local friend in Thomas Woodburne, who lived in the Crake Valley. His daughter Kitty was two years younger than Joyce, and often came to play; after the death of both her parents in 1899, she would come to live with Edith Ransome. They also brought friends with them from Leeds. A *Westmorland Gazette* notice preserved in Arthur's cutting book records that 'Professor Ransome and his family, Mr and Mrs Eddison and Mr Hubbersty – all from Leeds – took up their residence in Laurel House, High Nibthwaite for September.' Three years older than Arthur, Eric Eddison was an excellent companion in mischief and literary imagination. His uncle was Andrew Lang, the great collector of fairy tales, and Eric himself wrote fantasy novels, most famously *The Worm Ouroboros*, which begins in Wasdale. John Hubbersty, son of the Vicar of Cartmel, was a solicitor in Leeds, married to Edith's sister Mabel.

The greatest treat was a day spent rowing up the lake to Peel Island, so steep-sided that it looked like a floating fortress, and so densely wooded that its heart was a jungle of greenery. 'We landed in the lovely little harbour at the south end and spent the day as savages. My mother would settle down to make a sketch in watercolours. My father, forgetting to eat his sandwiches, would drift far along the lake-shores, casting his flies, and coming back in the evening with trout in the bottom of the boat for Mrs Swainson to cook for next day's breakfast.'

In 1892, Cyril stumbled in the river while fishing at Spark Bridge. The injury developed into a tubercular infection. First his foot and then his shin had to be amputated, but he acquired a cork prosthesis and continued to shoot and fish. Four years later, Peel Island was the scene of an encounter with a significant aftermath. William Gershom ('WG') Collingwood (1854–1932), archaeologist and Norse scholar, was secretary to John Ruskin. The Collingwoods lived in Lanehead, a mile further north. WG had excavated Peel Island and found traces of a Viking settlement on it, and in 1895 he published *Thorstein of the Mere*, a thrilling Viking romance set around Coniston. Thorstein, the young hero, goes to ground on Peel Island when he is being hunted by his enemies. Just before Christmas, WG received a fan letter from Cyril Ransome, who had known him at Oxford.

Dear Collingwood,

On behalf of four small children, Arthur, Cecily, Geoffrey & Joyce, who have from their earliest recollections been accustomed to regard Nibthwaite and Coniston as a fairyland of pleasant memories and delightful holidays, I wish to thank you for your *Thorstein of the Mere*. Every member of the family old and young has read it with the utmost pleasure and interest, and we are looking forward to re-visiting all the scenes of his adventures with renewed enthusiasm next August which we generally spend with perhaps some of his descendants, the Swainsons of Nibthwaite.

WG sent him an offprint of his paper 'The Vikings in Lakeland' and suggested a meeting on Peel Island in the summer of 1896. After they had picnicked together, Mrs Collingwood noted in her diary that the Ransome children were disappointingly plain, given their charming parents. Cyril and WG continued to correspond over the winter, by which time Cyril had decided that he would like to run for Parliament.

Early in 1897, he moved his family to Rugby, planning to be a sixth-form tutor while looking for a seat. Arthur, still at prep school in Windermere, was put in for the Rugby scholarship exam; when he arrived to take it, he found his father desperately ill. Unsurprisingly, Arthur failed the exam lamentably, but was given a place at Rugby as a day boy. His father died a few weeks later, aged only forty-six. Grandfather Tom Ransome died in the same year aged seventy-two. Their deaths were a considerable double trauma for a boy of thirteen.

Although Edith went on taking the children on imaginative holidays (Scarborough, Wiltshire, Wales, as well as visits to north country relatives, and to Finsthwaite, near the southern end of Windermere) the magical times at Nibthwaite ended. But they remained enshrined in Arthur's memory. It is not far-fetched to

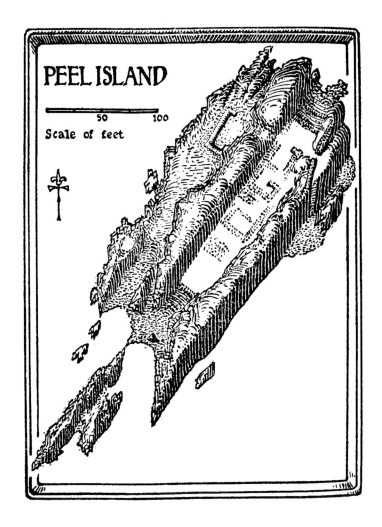

see conscious homage to Cyril in his decision at forty-five, about the same age that Cyril was when he died, to write *Swallows and Amazons*, a book in which he lovingly recreated the world of his childhood holidays on Coniston Water.

OPPOSITE Peel Island: *Arbeia* in the 'secret harbour', and the path up to the camp

ABOVE
LEFT Map of Peel Island, by W. G. Collingwood
RIGHT Frontispiece from W. G. Collingwood's
Thorstein of the Mere

THE LITERARY APPRENTICE

'Brave dreams flooded my mind, and I sat content long after it was dusk and smoked,
and sent with infinite enjoyment puffs of pale smoke out into the night. I did not go to
bed at all, but fell asleep leaning on the window sill, to wake with a cold in my head.'

Arthur Ransome, Autobiography

Ransome's children's books never pall because no two of them are the same; they are never churned out to a formula. Each one is a unique construction, with its own individual emphasis; sometimes on characters, sometimes on action, sometimes a traditional quest, sometimes a mystery to be solved. The twelve books are in themselves an education in the art of storytelling – which is exactly what he underwent during the ten years after his father died.

Arthur enjoyed his four years at Rugby, especially once his extreme short-sightedness had been detected and corrected with spectacles. During his first two terms as a day boy, his talent as a writer was spotted and encouraged by his form-master, the scholarly polyglot W. H. Rouse, whose love of folklore, sailing and sea shanties Arthur came to share. He made some lasting friends, most notably Ted Scott, son of the editor of the *Manchester Guardian*, and Philip Rouse, with whom he would have the happiest sailing days of his life.

He remained a voracious reader, racing through Spenser's *Faerie Queen*, relishing 'the limpid Greek of the New Testament' and reading 'a good deal of Shakespeare, a good deal of Carlyle, a lot of Stevenson, and every book of folk tales I could get my hands on'. Rouse offered to tutor Arthur for Oxford, but though Arthur already longed to be a creative writer, he felt responsible for supporting his mother and turned instead to science, winning a place to read chemistry at Leeds' Yorkshire College in 1901. He was only seventeen.

Living alone in lodgings was a liberating experience. 'I was free in a new sense. There were good bookshops in Leeds and my allowance of pocket money, that would have been ridiculously inadequate at Oxford, allowed me, who had no expensive tastes, to buy books, cheap ones, without disapproval from anyone.' Looking for a book on magnetism, he happened on J. W. Mackail's *Life of William Morris*, dipped into it and forgot his laboratory work.

'I read entranced of the lives of the young Morris and his friends, of lives in which nothing seemed to matter except the making of lovely things and the making of a world to match them.' Arthur read and reread the book, drinking up its descriptions of Kelmscott Manor and excursions on the Thames, and his dream of being a writer surfaced unstoppably. Aware that shifting to the Arts faculty would postpone his ability to earn his own living, he decided to get a job in which he could at least work with books. His mother tried to discourage him, but in February 1902 he applied for a job as an office boy with the London publisher Grant Richards. Edith went to London herself in order to call on Grant Richards and take soundings from Maurice Macmillan and Thomas Longman, who published Cyril's textbooks; then resigned herself to what she rightly thought a very risky undertaking.

Ransome's eight shillings a week were more than enough to pay for board and lodging with distant relatives in Clapham, with money over to buy books galore from stalls in the Charing Cross Road. He called on his much older cousin Laurence Binyon, now

LEFT The happily bespectacled Arthur at Rugby
RIGHT 67 Huron Road, Balham, Ransome's London home in 1902

in his mid-thirties and an established poet. Through Laurence's good offices, Arthur got an undemanding job for £1 a week as 'assistant' at Binyon's own publisher, the Unicorn Press in Cecil Court, off St Martin's Lane. This gave him time to supplement his income with articles on 'anything for which I could find a market', and to continue his intense programme of self-education in literature. He began to meet authors: the Yeats brothers, Bram Stoker, J. M. Barrie, Cecil and G. K. Chesterton, and Edith Nesbit, whose children's books influenced his own. He was fascinated by the West Indian fantasy writer M. P. Shiel, and 'Pixie' Colman Smith, who grew up in Jamaica and whose illustrated tellings of Jamaican folklore, *Annancy Stories*, was published in 1902. Ransome thought her 'god-daughter to a witch and sister to a fairy', and was fascinated by the way she told these tales of an intrepid and resourceful spider. 'I learnt more of the art of narrative from these simple folk-tales than ever from any book.' His true kindred

spirits were, however, such thoroughly English writers as Gordon Bottomley, John Masefield and Edward Thomas, with whom he would pace for miles across the Kent and Hampshire hills.

In the autumn of 1902, his mother and sisters arrived in London. Geoffrey had gone into a boarding house at Rugby, and Cecily was to go to art school. Arthur joined them in a spacious house in Huron Road, Balham that Edith had rented, proud to offer ten shillings towards his keep. He relished its home comforts, especially returning home late at night to find Joyce's governess

mulling nutmeg-flavoured claret for him. Geoffrey came home for the holidays, and he and Arthur enjoyed jaunts to the theatre; free tickets were in endless supply at the Unicorn Press. Arthur was a little in awe of his clever younger brother, who teased him, as the whole family did, about his distinctly Bohemian appearance.

In August 1903 he decided he could afford a place of his own. He found a large square corner room two storeys above a Chelsea grocer's shop, commandeered a horse-drawn van to transport his chattels (largely books) from Balham and rode proudly away on its tailboard to 'a place of my own choosing, to be an absolutely free man. I doubt if any young man at university living in comparative comfort can ever know the happiness that was mine at nineteen, dependent solely on what I was able to earn and living in a room of my own with the books I had myself collected.'

The room was like the bridge of a ship, with windows on to Fawcett Street and Hollywood Road. It was unfurnished, with dull grey-green walls and no form of lighting. Water had to be carried up from the ground floor, and the landlord was suspicious of his new lodger's lack of worldly goods. Ransome saw the room through rose-tinted spectacles. 'I was free to live for poetry, for philosophy, for all the things that seemed then to matter more than life itself.' After unloading his books, he shopped for food: apples, bread and cheese, with beer to wash all down. For furniture he acquired 'three shillings-worth of indifferently clean packing cases'. He arranged some as table and chairs, and stacked two on their sides as a cupboard. Three more put end to end 'made an admirable bed', which a railway rug 'gave an air of comfort, even opulence'. He sat at the window to read a book of ballads by the fading light and listen to the sounds of the city: the mournful hoot of a river steamer, the bells of churches, passers-by in the street, even a noisy argument in the room below added to his sense of adventure.

In later years, Ransome would lament that he had as a young man sacrificed his stomach to his library, eating unhealthy and irregular meals at street stalls, taverns and Soho coffee houses, snacking on sandwiches and bananas, or simply skipping food altogether in favour of acquiring another literary treasure. His cookery skills were inventive but basic.

> A solid meal could be made from a haddock and the cooking of it wasted no time. Haddocks could be bought in the King's Road. I used to buy my haddock and take it home, then boil a kettle of water on the fire, and pour the boiling water over the haddock in a saucepan, put the lid on, read for another ten minutes, when a meal would be ready that would last for twenty-four hours.

Early in 1904, Ransome moved to a handsome ground-floor front room in Gunter Grove. The rent was eight shillings a week, which included breakfast and the cost of lamps, coal and laundry. Edward Thomas later described Arthur's domestic arrangements in a letter to their mutual friend Gordon Bottomley.

> He has quite a good room with a bed delicately suggested by a tapestry cover, and other things suggested by a Japanese screen. His books, some portraits, drawings by Coleman-Smith, and some of Balmer's, and on the mantelpiece some of the drawings of 'An I[mportant] P[erson]' and a great bulk of the landlady's glass and china decorations and in the midst of it a large earthenware pot with tap containing ginger beer which his visitors always spill into his landlady's fender and onto her Japanese umbrella which conceals the fireplace.

In August 1904, a parcel arrived from Ulverston, which Ransome opened 'with shaking hands'. In it were six copies of his first 'real' book, *The Souls in the Streets and Other Little Papers*, published by the Lanthorn Press. Sixty years later, Ransome still vividly recalled his pride in it: 'I can remember patting its silly little cover much as I have patted a boat when she and I have been alone at sea and struggling along in unkindly weather.'

The Lanthorn Press was the brainchild of Gordon Bottomley, who then lived at Well Knowe, in Cartmel. Early in 1904, he had invited Ransome to visit him there to plan books for the Lanthorn to publish, and this return to the north altered Ransome's life. In later visits to Cartmel, he stayed at Wall Nook, where he met Lascelles Abercrombie, who was like him struggling to make writing his métier, and who became a lifelong friend. But the greatest attraction of all was a gracious white house overlooking Coniston Water called Lanehead.

LEFT Wall Nook, Cartmel, where Ransome spent three summer holidays between 1904 and 1906
RIGHT A vivid 1908 sketch of Arthur Ransome by his friend Alphaeus Cole (1876–1988)

LANEHEAD AND THE COLLINGWOODS

'A little advice on the technique of literature given by a master to a young man
may dictate his career, not only as an artist, but as a man.'
Arthur Ransome, *'Maeterlinck and Symbolism',* The Bookman, *26 October 1911*

A year earlier, in June 1903, Arthur had decided that he could afford what would be his first holiday since he had left Rugby. He knew exactly where he would take it. Jumping on a night train from Euston, he changed at Carnforth and took the Furness railway to Coniston. There he took lodgings in Bank House (now the Yewdale Hotel). Having performed his customary rite of dipping his hand in the lake, he walked up the Coppermines Valley towards the Old Man. Seeing a fine flat rock dividing the beck, he jumped across to it, lay down, pulled out a notebook and closed his eyes in preparation for poetic inspiration. Then came a happy piece of happenstance. W. G. Collingwood was coming down the fellside after a painting session. He saw Arthur's prone body and called out to see if he was injured. 'I told him I had been trying to write poetry,' Ransome recalled. 'Instead of laughing, he seemed to think it a reasonable occupation.' When Collingwood realized that the would-be-bard was Cyril Ransome's son Arthur, the boy whom he and his wife had met seven years earlier on Peel Island, they invited him to visit them.

Shyness made Arthur put off his visit to Lanehead until the last days of his holiday, when he was awed to find himself dining with William Canton, famous for his fairy tales. The Collingwoods' fourteen-year-old son Robin had just won a scholarship to Rugby; Ransome could not only tell them all about the school but suggest an introduction to his brother Geoffrey, now in his second year. Ransome called on Robin at his prep school in Grange, and chatted to him about Rugby, and Collingwood gave Ransome his

1899 *Coniston Tales*, inscribed 'With the Author's compliments and thanks. Coniston, July 10, 1903'.

In May 1904, Arthur visited Rugby and took Robin and Geoffrey out to tea, on his way north to Coniston. This time he called at Lanehead immediately. WG invited him in to his study.

> I can see it now, the books from floor to ceiling, the enormous long table piled with books and manuscripts, the unfinished canvas on an easel, the small table at which he was writing and, over the fireplace, his lovely portrait of his wife, in a small boat with two of the children. He put me in one armchair, shifted his own from the table and asked about what I was doing. The miracle was his assumption that what I was trying to do was worthwhile.

The more Arthur and WG talked, the more they realized how much they had in common. WG was also heart and soul in love with the Lake Country, which he first discovered through his Liverpool-based family's holidays at Gillhead, on Windermere. He too had faced family opposition to his choice of career, but had succeeded in the chancy occupation of artist thanks to the support of John Ruskin, through whom he had met Edward Burne-Jones. He too admired William Morris and loved poetry, folk tales and history. Through painting, geological and archaeological expeditions, he knew the Lake Country like the back of his hand. In 1893 he had written an introduction to Coniston-born John

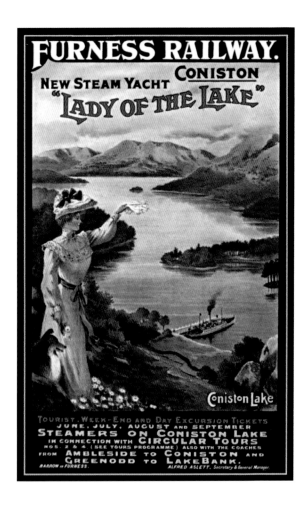

Beever's *Practical Fly-Fishing Founded on Nature*, a book that Ransome would, forty years later, include in a list of his favourite fishing books. Like Ransome, WG was resourceful and inventive, helping Ruskin build a pier at Brantwood for his boat, *Jumping Jenny*, and constructing a huge globe at Coniston School into which the children could clamber to observe the stars.

Lanehead had been the Collingwood family home since 1891. Built in 1848 on the site of an old inn, and extended three years later, it boasted a dozen rooms, a conservatory, a studio loft above its stable block and a large flower-filled garden edged with rhododendrons and pines, behind which a field sloped down to boathouses and the lake. There was a vegetable garden, an

orchard and a poultry yard. The younger Collingwood children, Robin and Ursula, were away at school, but the older girls, Dora (eighteen) and Barbara (seventeen), were at home; their cousin Hilde was also staying.

On the day he arrived, Arthur rowed them across to Coniston in a venerable old dinghy called *Swallow*. After a few days of returning to his Coniston digs at night, he was invited to stay in Robin's bedroom, and to work in a small downstairs room next to WG's study. From then on until his return to London he lived in a golden haze. The household woke to Mrs Collingwood's early morning piano practice; then came breakfast and a run down to the lake and back. Then the house was silent. WG worked in

OPPOSITE
LEFT 1908 poster advertising a new Coniston
steam yacht; Peel Island is visible in the distance
RIGHT Barbara Collingwood, Ransome's own 'lady
of the lake'

LEFT
ABOVE Lanehead today, showing the fir trees at the
end of the garden
BELOW Lanehead in 1893, by Ransome's mentor
W. G. Collingwood (1854–1932)

his study; Ransome in his allotted room or the library; Dorrie in her studio. The girls worked at their easels or with clay in the Mausoleum, a conservatory, chilly in winter, that was used as a second studio.

After lunch 'we younger ones would go forth with bun-loaf and kettle, to sketch and read in the open air, to make our fire by the shore of the lake . . . then, as it grew dark, we would come into the big morning-room that was always full of flowers'. Dorrie would play again, and they sang and told stories in front of the fire; Arthur specialized in West Indian 'Anansi' tales.

Ransome returned year after year, confiding in WG and Dorrie, falling in love with first Barbara and then Dora, learning to sail in *Swallow*, little *Toob* and a larger boat called *Jamrach*. His experiences with the older generations of the Collingwood family played as great a part as his observation of Dora's five children in the creation of what has aptly been called the 'saga' of the Swallows and Amazons. Just as Collingwood's *Thorstein* paid tribute to the first Norse settlers in the Lakes, so Ransome paid tribute to modern invaders like his own family and the Collingwoods. He larded his books with a host of in-jokes, which Dora called in a letter 'the secret japes and details that your general public doesn't know anything about'. The patterans that the Swallows leave to mark their route to the Amazons' house, Beckfoot, were in common use on Collingwood family walks, and the four fir trees that identify Beckfoot to the Swallows as they tramp across the moor from Swallowdale were a favourite reading retreat in the Lanehead garden.

'The first of a long line of Swallows': this 1905 photo shows Ursula Collingwood at the helm

BOHEMIAN AT LARGE

*'It was interest in French storytellers that sent me to Paris. I had a few pounds in hand,
and told myself that I had better go now, in case I never have so much again.'*

Arthur Ransome, Autobiography

Running in parallel with Ransome's visits to Lanehead was a hectic round of literary activity in London and in Paris. He first went to Paris late in 1904. The extended Ransome family produced a useful contact in Clive Bell, a clever young Cambridge graduate and later a star of the Bloomsbury set. He was studying in Paris, and his mother was a friend of one of Ransome's Wiltshire aunts. He recommended the Hôtel de la Haute Loire (now Hôtel Raspail) on the junction between Boulevard Raspail and rue Montparnasse, and Arthur took a cheap but chilly attic room on its seventh storey. He visited the Louvre with Bell, 'looking first for all the Poussins and Lorraines that had meant so much to William Hazlitt'.

Returning penniless to Gunter Grove, he felt that 'the door was ajar into a new world and that I had set my foot there so that it should not close again'. On his next visit to Paris, Bell took him to a funfair. They rode on a carousel, and sipped absinthe in Montmartre. Though he admired Bell enormously, he did not feel intellectually kin to him. 'His was the Paris of Mallarmé, mine that of Balzac and Gautier.' Arthur's sister Joyce regarded Bell with less awe. 'He is a limp, idiotic youth,' she wrote in her diary in August 1906. 'Very clever, but inordinately conceited. He writes, and spends the whole day over one sentence.' She was fourteen.

In 1906, the publishers T. & E. Jack commissioned Ransome to produce *The World's Storytellers,* a series of short-story collections by influential authors, mainly French, each with an introduction. His expenses would be advanced on account of royalties. He set off again to Paris, renting a cheap studio on the seventh floor of a block of ateliers in rue Campagne Première. He acquired 'a narrow box-mattress for a bed, a kitchen table on which to work, and a pleasant little iron stove that burned charcoal or *boulets* and more than once came near to closing my career by asphyxiation'. Soon he had his favourite haunts, including a restaurant in the Boulevard Raspail that gave him a special rate as he was such a regular customer, and the Seine-side bookstalls, where he turned over 'book after book, talking as it were for a moment with veteran after veteran, browned, scarred, and mellowed by travail with the world'.

Volumes on Edgar Allan Poe and E. T. A. Hoffman for T. & E. Jack's *World's Storytellers* series: Ransome introduced and chose the stories

LEFT Ransome's ground-floor flat at
1 Gunter Grove, Chelsea

RIGHT Ransome's *Highways & Byways
in Fairyland* (1910), *The Imp, The Elf
and The Ogre* (1910) and *Bohemia in
London* (1907)

When in London, as well as writing stories of his own and reviewing, Ransome was a publisher's reader. Early in 1906 he was asked to revive the flagging fortunes of *Temple Bar*, an old-fashioned journal that folded at the end of the year, despite Ransome's energetic commissioning of work from Edward Thomas, Gordon Bottomley, W. G. Collingwood and Lascelles Abercrombie. He wrote three little nature books for children, which were published in November 1906, and later appeared in one volume as *The Imp, The Elf and The Ogre* (1910). That year he also wrote *Highways and Byways in Fairyland*. For all its crimson boats and pigmy boatmen, elfin bells and gnome banqueting halls deep in the mountains, Ransome's Fairyland is recognizably the north country, with Hills of Longing, the Dreaming River, green larchwoods, grey rocks, waving bracken and a broad lake, deep and calm.

Towards the end of 1906, he met Stefana Stevens, a young literary agent at Curtis Brown. Both were then deep in gypsy lore. Ransome was reviewing George Borrow's *The Romany Rye* and Elizabeth Pennell's life of the folklorist Charles Godfrey Leland, and Stefana was studying Romany. Shrewdly assessing both the vigour and immediacy of his writing and the range of his acquaintance, she commissioned him to write 'an essayistical sort of book putting Bohemia of today against a background of the past'. He set to work at once. The result was *Bohemia in London* (1907), packed with literary history and lively pen portraits veiled under pseudonyms, and an effervescent narrator who was unmistakably Ransome himself.

Stefana satirized the Arthur of 1907 as Dicky Matravers in her 1916 novel *And What Happened*. 'In print he is the most fastidious and meticulous creature. In person he is bombastic, Gargantuan, thunderous, explosive, brutal and bouncing . . . His shagginess was not so much due to hairiness, for his face was smooth, except for an untidy and somewhat undeveloped moustache, as to a general impression conveyed by his personality. Possibly his aura was

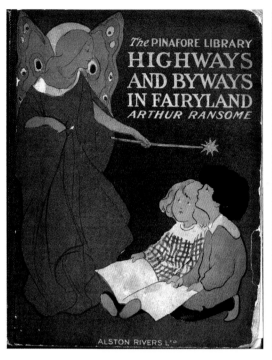

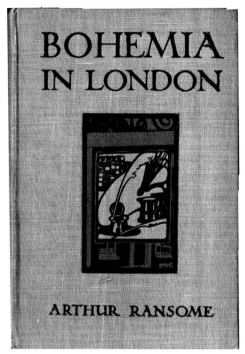

shaggy. He wore a worn old shooting jacket, a yellow tie, leggings, and an enormous pair of boots; altogether Letty had never seen a man more unsuitably attired for the London streets.'

Matravers' room is a portrait of Ransome's Chelsea kingdom. 'Beside the mantelpiece hung a long pipe-rack in which were ranged every imaginable pipe . . . Two sketches of Matravers's own head hung above the mantelpiece and a caricature of him smoking an enormous Russian pipe by the window.' 'Beaming, huge and shy', Matravers proudly exhibits the bookshelves he has made himself to replace the 'sugar boxes, they used to be kept in'. A silver loving cup is filled with wild daffodils ('Aren't they jolly? I bought them off a gypsy at Hammersmith this morning'). He presses his own books *Fauns and Fountains* and *Grassy Highways* on visitors, and shows off the treasures of his library: 'Here's my Boccaccio; isn't it a ripping edition? Here's a first edition of *The Farmers Boy*. Here's a Latin *Imitation of Christ*, with jolly little steel engravings. Look at this fellow beating his breast. Here's a

funny eighteenth century sermon on witch-craft. Here are some Elzevirs that belonged to my father.'

Within two days of meeting Letty, Matravers proposes to her (a tendency also much in character). After she refuses him, he disappears. Then a parcel arrives, and she recognizes his small, neat handwriting. Inside, a letter explains the contents:

Moss for the smell. If I was asked what romance smells of, I should say three things – moss on a wet day, a tarred rope on a sunny day, and wood-smoke at all times. That for one of your senses, then. Primroses and the rest for touch – they are fresher and sweeter than those the flower-women sell. I picked them this morning before breakfast. The eggs to remind you of country hedges and what all good birds are about just now. I wish I could send you a little of the concert they favour me with every morning. The plovers' eggs will

THE WORLD OF ARTHUR RANSOME

please Nico, who is greedy. I found them on the moor between here and Dykeham after carefully watching a plover to see where it came to earth. They are hard-boiled. The watercresses were sold to me by a gypsy five minutes ago. The stone is the most valuable thing in the box. Don't ever let it pass out of your possession. It is very rare to find a black kidney-shaped stone, and is one of the luckiest talismans one can possibly possess. I've been looking for one for years. When will you marry me?

Although Ransome enjoyed urban Bohemianism, his favourite authors were still Hazlitt, Masefield and Stevenson and his heart inclined most to friends with whom he could combine walking and talking. The Lakes remained magnetically attractive. Whenever he could, he sped north to see the Collingwoods, or to stay at Wall Nook, the farmhouse near Cartmel. In 1908 Ransome based himself at the Bennetts' farm at Low Yewdale, at the head of the Coniston Valley, under Raven Crag. He was amalgamating his *World's Storytellers* prefaces into *A History of Story-Telling*, a book that reveals his profound understanding of the tools of his chosen trade. When it was fine he camped in his 'King's Herdsman' tent, a simple design with heavy canvas suspended over two pairs of slanted poles, their tips protruding 'like rabbits' ears' at each end, which he acquired in 1908.

Rather to the horror of the Bennetts, Ransome encouraged visits from Lake Country gypsies. Travelling showmen and tinkers, many still spoke the Romany language that had fascinated Arthur since reading Borrow. He played pickpocket games ('much better than poker') with them in local inns, and heard about the gypsy centre at Millom 'where all the old buck Romans go in the winters to sit by the fire'. Interestingly, he never introduces gypsies into his children's books, but in his autobiography he brackets them with the charcoal-burners, the Swainsons of Nibthwaite and the Towers of Wall Nook as 'old friends who helped to make me feel that I had a countryside I could call my own. I valued them for their own sake, and, as I valued the corncrakes in the fields below the bobbin mill, the heron by the lake-shore and the otters sporting by moonlight in the lake, as proofs to myself that I had again come home.'

Visiting friends called to admire his camp: Lascelles Abercrombie and his girlfriend Catherine Gwatkin, Jan Gordon (an art critic) and his fiancée Miss Turner, and Dixon Scott, once a protégé of Bottomley but now critical of the preciousness of some of the Well Knowe set. Scott declared that their own watchword should be 'Roast Beef and Rosebuds'. He liked Ransome's tent so much that he bought one for himself, pitching it on Wansfell, above Skelgill. Still very close to his own family, Ransome also used to walk over Walna Scar to the Duddon Valley, where Edith Ransome was holidaying in Ulpha with Geoffrey, Cecily and Joyce.

Ransome beside his 'second home', a 'King's Herdsman' tent, which he boasted was 'one of the first to be seen in the valley'

RANSOME IN LOVE

*'Falling in love with love is the one illogical adventure, the one thing of which we are
tempted to think as supernatural, in our trite and reasonable world.'*

Robert Louis Stevenson, Virginibus Puerisque

What of romance? The heady freedom of a room of his own naturally led Arthur to look around for feminine company, especially after 1905, when the protective womenfolk of his own family moved to Edinburgh, so that they could keep house for Geoffrey, now apprenticed to a printer there. Cyril had treated Edith as an equal, and Ransome, who relished the independent spirit of his sisters and the other young women he met in London's literary and artistic circles, hoped to achieve a similar marriage of true minds. 'It was not that I had fallen in love with anybody,' he admitted in his autobiography, 'merely that I wanted some sort of reassurance, and that I wanted to have someone at the other end of the breakfast-table, to walk with, to make a home with and, using Hazlitt's phrase, perfectly expressive of this kind of domesticity, someone with whom "to gather mushrooms to drop into our hashed mutton".'

During his second visit to Lanehead, the one that extended into a holiday, he believed he had found what the poet Richard Crashaw famously called 'That not impossible She'. Dora Collingwood's diary maps the gradual development of a romance between Arthur and her sister Barbara. 'Last Saturday Mr Ransome came to dinner. He is staying in the village and has been to dinner every day since,' Dora wrote on 3 June 1904. 'He is coming to stay with us tomorrow.'

Ransome was then busy with his first book, *The Souls of the Streets*, which he sent piecemeal to the Ulverston printers from Lanehead, and Barbara helped in reading the galleys. 'Mrs Collingwood, finding her busy with them, laughed and said, "You

have got the beginnings of an intelligent public already"' is the first hint of the romance in his autobiography, which says little more, but Dora's diary reveals that Barbara was the 'I.P.' to whom *Souls* was dedicated, and whose drawing had a place of honour on his Gunter Grove mantelpiece.

Next summer Ransome stayed at Wall Nook, but he mentions walking over via the Rusland Valley and Lowick 'to see Barbara', and in the August 1905 issue of the Collingwoods' family magazine, 'What-Ho!', there is a poem by Arthur, written in Barbara's handwriting:

> I will make a necklace of amethyst and emerald,
> I will make a necklace, to fasten on her throat,
> And in the moonlight, out in the moonlight,
> In the summer moonlight we'll go sailing in a boat.

> I will make a ringlet of gold and red cornelian,
> I will make a ringlet, and feel her little hand
> Fluttering in mine as I fit upon her finger,
> On her little finger a gold and scarlet band.

After much havering, Barbara turned him down. Arthur began to play the field in London. 'He is just resting after his sixth (serious) affair of the heart', Edward Thomas wrote of him to Bottomley in January 1906. Soon afterwards he began the flirtation with Stefana Stevens that she affectionately describes in *And What Happened*. Another object of his all too easily bestowed affection was a pretty young Liverpudlian called Jessie Gavin, whom he met in Paris. She was an accomplished etcher, and he asked her to illustrate his *World's Storytellers*. She shared his love of the Lakes ('with her I felt that the north country was never far away'), and soon he was in love. They took the train out to Rambouillet and went for long tramps in the forest, feasting on *oeufs brouillés* at a little inn before going back to Paris.

Were Jessie and Arthur lovers? Probably not, although Paris was famously a city of sin, and many an upright young Englishman went there to divest himself of his virginity. In conservative minds, Bohemianism was synonymous with immorality, and it is true that Bohemians talked much of free love, and dismissed marriage as bondage. Children's authors are not immune to passion. Ransome's contemporaries Edith Nesbit, Enid Bagnold and Kathleen Hale were all, like the heroine of Grant Richards' notorious 1895 novel, 'women who did'. But Stevens made Matravers gallantly honourable, and it is likely that Arthur was like him in this as well as much else. Moreover, Jessie was not in love with him. 'I'm afraid it is too late to tell me not to fall in love with her,' he wrote to his mother. 'But I think I may leave Paris earlier than I otherwise should, because I think I shall be extremely unhappy. There is not the slightest chance that she will care for me, she is not at all the "You love me and I love you" kind of person. She is much more like a kind of fairy that does not seem approachable at all. And yet she is as sweet and charming as she can be.'

He was not, however, cast down when he returned to England in December, and raced north for Christmas with his family in Edinburgh. 'Arthur arrived at breakfast time', wrote Joyce in her diary for 13 December 1907. 'He left Paris on Tuesday night, and had spent two days in London. He was wearing a Norfolk suit, a corduroy waistcoat, a squash hat, and instead of a muffler, he had a yard of pale mauve Japanese silk round his neck and he evidently hadn't shaved for days. He went and had a bath as soon as he arrived. He is in very good spirits and looks extremely well.'

Dora Collingwood in 1909

Next, Arthur began to think that perhaps Dora was the girl of his dreams. A close reading of her diary makes it clear that she had long wondered the same. Ever since she had met him in May 1904, she had recorded every sighting she had of him, both at Lanehead and in the London flat that he found for the Collingwoods close to his own lodgings. In the summer of 1908, they spent a great deal of time together picnicking, walking and sailing. These were the days of the tent near Low Yewdale, and a contemporary photograph shows a bespectacled Dora in white blouse with leg-of-mutton sleeves smiling shyly up at the camera beside it. They had just finished tea out of Arthur's new tea basket, of which he was immensely proud. She recorded the occasion in her diary. 'I did enjoy it so much. He was very nice, he is so utterly different from any man I know – indeed he is the only one I know well, and in spite of his many eccentricities he really is a dear.' Looking up at her leaning out of a Lanehead window to chat to him a few days later, he said, 'Talking to you is like eating

ABOVE Camping at Yewdale, showing (left) Dora and (right) Arthur outside his tent
LEFT Page from Dora's diary for 1908, showing coded writing

Tuesday. morning.

Very wet.
Yesterday was showery. I spent all the morning clearing out Robin's room, & making it into a bedroom. Miss Comber came to tea. letter fr ORC Sunday. wet. wrote to Ursula. went to tea with Mrs Hipwell at Tent Lodge.
This evening we began reading "Caesar 'de Bello Gallico." for Reading Entrance Examination. No more Greek, alas!
Mother & Robin went to Lee-on-Solent yesterday.

The longest Day   Wednesday. 21st
Today began by being dull & stormy, but after breakfast it cleared up and became quite bright. The mountains were the most glorious dark blue, & the bracken bright green, and the becks were very full of white water. I painted & sat for B. to paint me all the morning; in the afternoon Mr & Mrs Mills came to look at the house,

but I don't think they'll take it ——— when they'd gone I did a spell of painting. After tea B & I went to call on Miss Hilliard. then for a walk.

Today at last we got a letter from Mother. She won't be back for ages yet. I do hate ordering meals — I'd rather scrub floors.

Thursday. 22nd.
Fine, very hot — began by being dull. Painted all the morning. & B paints me in the afternoon - after tea we went on to lake. & read the history of ...

strawberry ice.' She entered the compliment in her diary, which at this time often breaks into a secret code that no one has yet deciphered.

A month later, while sitting for his portrait in the Lanehead studio, he asked her to marry him. Perhaps because she still vividly recalled his courtship of Barbara, perhaps because he had confided his feelings for Jessie to her, perhaps because she suspected that they were not in truth well suited, she refused. 'I don't think he was serious. He seems to want to marry anyone and everyone – anything for a wife,' she wrote shrewdly, and perhaps sadly, in her diary.

When Ransome returned to London, he moved into a second-floor flat in Owen Mansions, his grandest quarters yet, reflecting his growing prosperity. 'I had there a good workroom, plenty of bookshelves, the first of the big tables I have always liked, two armchairs, one given me by my mother, a kitchen, airy bedroom, a bathroom, and a "daily woman" who used to come in the mornings to tidy up, though I did most of my own cooking.' He proposed to Dora again in December, when she visited him there, but made the mistake of hinting that she had a rival. 'I ignored everything he said and urged him to go to the other damsel and ask her,' she wrote. 'I wish he would make up his mind. I'm sure he would make a lot of money if he had some object to work for. As things are, he thinks too much about himself . . . and he is much too young to retire to the country.' Clearly she had the shrewd suspicion that Arthur was more in love with the idea of being one of the Collingwood family than with either Barbara or herself. What he saw in Lanehead was the most wonderful home imaginable, a place where all he achieved was praised instead of laughed at or doubted, a place where he could relive the abruptly ended holidays of his childhood.

ABOVE Double sketch of Ransome by Dora Collingwood, c.1908
BELOW Ransome's most spacious flat was 7 Owen Mansions, part of the 1892 Queen's Club Gardens development in Baron's Court

THE MARRIED MAN

'My opinion of love is, that it acts upon the human heart
precisely as a nutmeg-grater acts upon a nutmeg.'
Percy Bysshe Shelley, quoted by Arthur Ransome in The Book of Love

At about the time that Arthur was giving up hope of capturing one of the ladies of his own especial lake, a young American called Ralph Courtney visited Owen Mansions, bringing with him Ivy Constance Walker, a dark-haired pocket Venus with challenging brown eyes. Arthur was a ripe apple ready to drop. In all likelihood, she was the rival that Arthur mentioned to Dora in December. Flirtatious badinage and trips to the Earls Court roller-skating rink followed. Then Ivy announced that she was on the brink of unwillingly marrying a cousin, that the dress was already made, that she was desperate to escape from the engagement.

Strongly sexually attracted to Ivy, and revelling in the role of Young Lochinvar, Ransome rose to the occasion. 'On Saturday I heard from Arthur – who tells me that he is nearly engaged to a lady called Ivy who apparently is very charming and writes,' Dora recorded in her diary on 23 January 1909, adding, with understandable pique, 'It is all very sudden – a very short time ago his heart was in a very different place.' Their marriage took place in a register office on 13 March 1909. Arthur was twenty-five, Ivy twenty-six. They left for a two-week honeymoon in Paris on the same day. 'At the eleventh hour my mother decided to run away with my father – a Common Writer', wrote their only child, Tabitha, in a memoir written in her old age. 'My father had a Wild & Bohemian nature and lived an adventurous life in Paris with my mother.'

The Ransomes abandoned Owen Mansions for rural Surrey. Edward Thomas found them a cottage at Stonor Hill Top, half a mile from his own Berryfield Cottage, near Ashford. Arthur and Ivy arrived at the end of March, and stayed eight months. They were infatuated with each other. Tabitha remembers her father telling her that he and Ivy 'used to entwine like serpents on the lawn, and made love up an apple-tree'. Such a boast sounds more typical of Ivy, but there is no reason to doubt its truth.

But Ransome was as passionate about his work as he was about his wife. He settled down to finish his *History of Story-Telling*. Isolated in the country, Ivy was soon bored. One day she announced that her jilted fiancé was planning to abduct her, and told Arthur to

Studio portrait of Ivy
Constance Walker

LEFT From 1910 to 1911, Ransome was a regular contributor to
The Tramp magazine
RIGHT Ivy helped Arthur prepare his 1910 anthology *The Book of Love*

buy a revolver. Her fantasies multiplied. 'From one day to the next, I never knew what new form melodrama would take.' Ransome took her to Wall Nook, hoping she would love the north country as much as he did, but she lasted only three days, interpreting the plain-spoken ways of the folk of Furness as insolence.

Back in Surrey, Ransome began a punishing work schedule. In 1910 and 1911, he and Edward Thomas both contributed regularly to a sadly short-lived periodical called *The Tramp*, a magazine for literary-minded vagabonds which was ideally suited to their talents. His little *World's Storytellers* volumes were attracting acclaim, and Martin Secker, who was just setting up

as a publisher, commissioned a critical study of Edgar Allan Poe from him. Ransome also had to produce more *Storytellers* and compile two substantial anthologies of 'essays, poems, maxims and prose passages' for T. & E. Jack. These at least provided an opportunity for Ivy to work with him. He praised her 'incredible labours in transcribing and correcting' in the preface to *The Book of Friendship*, which was published soon after *The History of Story-Telling* in the autumn of 1909. The newly-weds worked equally closely on *The Book of Love* (1910), which was dedicated to Ivy. Its preface gives a touching picture of them working together.

There is a long room, whose walls are covered with books from floor to ceiling. The room has deep windows, and bowls on the broad window seats are full of flowers. A table is in the middle of the room, a step-ladder to reach the topmost shelves, and two

Christening portrait of Tabitha with Ivy,
November 1910

chairs for sedentary discussions. There is no doubt, however, that the top of the stepladder is the best seat of all, where the flies circle slowly between your head and the ceiling, and the books are close at hand . . . We walk up and down, smoking and observing the shelves, as you would watch a crowd in which you might have friends. Book after book reminds us of something which should find its place in the shadowy volume that is building in the air.

In November 1909, they moved back to London; Ivy was four months pregnant with Tabitha. Their domestic life was remarkably unsettled for the next year and a half. Carriers' carts loaded with books and baby paraphernalia were needed no fewer than eight times. Tabitha was born in Bournemouth on 9 May 1910. When she was six weeks old, they went north to show her to Arthur's family in Edinburgh, and stayed for six weeks. They returned south in August, and took lodgings in Milford, near Godalming, halfway between London and Bournemouth. Ransome began work on a critical study of Stevenson.

Towards the end of September, WG and Dorrie asked Arthur if he and Ivy would like to live at Lanehead after they had headed south for the autumn term at Reading, where WG was now teaching. He accepted gratefully, and arranged for Ivy and Tabitha to join him early in October. Shortly after they had arrived, with a comfortable Jamaican nanny, a telegram from Secker announced that he wanted Ransome to write a critical study of Oscar Wilde before the Stevenson, because it would sell better. Ransome agreed regretfully, and Secker posted Wilde's complete works to him.

Ransome also found time to write numerous articles and to pen some essays and fey stories of his own, inspired by proverbs (one was 'A Rolling Stone Gathers No Moss'). Two longer stories, both set in the Lake Country, 'The Ageing Faun' and 'Peter Swainson', joined

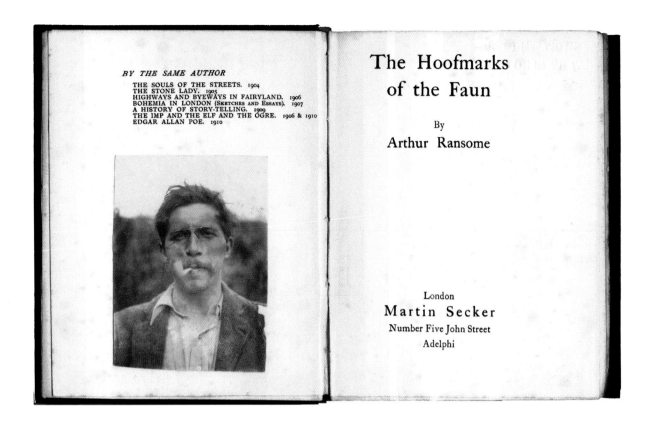

The Hoofmarks of the Faun

By
Arthur Ransome

London
Martin Secker
Number Five John Street
Adelphi

A characterful photograph of Ransome was pasted into this presentation copy of his first book of fiction, *The Hoofmarks of the Faun* (1911)

four earlier stories that he had written to make up another little book of his own work, *Hoofmarks of the Faun*, which was published in April 1911. Two tales were dedicated to Ivy, one to Dora (dated Chelsea 1904) and one to Barbara (dated 1905). Although fey and flawed, they have some lovely Lake Country details.

When he was not writing, Arthur was 'sailing on the lake, collecting from the Red Lion at Lowick the clay pipes, blackened by their fires, that my old friends the charcoal-burners had left there for me, and walking to the Duddon, to Windermere, to Cartmel, by the old well-known roads'. What was Ivy doing? Perhaps she went on at least some of the day-long tramps that Ransome mentions, and also sailed on occasion, but his diary makes no mention of her doing so. Towards the end of October, they both went to Paris, leaving Tabitha with the nanny, so that Arthur could research Wilde's years there in the 1890s. They

returned in early November, and Tabitha was christened in Coniston Church. They went back to London in mid-December, and went straight to Paris for Christmas, again without Tabitha. They returned to London in February.

Quite why the Ransomes' life should have been nomadic for so long is not clear. They moved nine times in the first two years of their marriage, to say nothing of visits to friends and relatives, and to Paris. Funds grew scarce. Hiring a resident nanny and providing domestic help for Ivy was much more expensive than living in bachelor digs looked after by a landlady. The advent of the baby and the many moves meant that Ransome did not have time to produce the usual blizzard of articles, signed and unsigned, with which he normally tided himself over while researching longer books. But at last they found a house that felt as if it fitted them like a glove.

LOVE IN A COTTAGE

*'I was just as far from being a husband of the kind she would have chosen as she was
from being a suitable wife for me. It is unfair to tell any such story from one side only.'*

Arthur Ransome, letter to Rupert Hart-Davis, 1961

On 26 April 1911, Arthur and Ivy viewed Manor Farm, in the hamlet of Hatch, a mile from Tisbury, in Wiltshire. Built of worn grey limestone from the ruins of a monastery, it was tile-roofed with mullioned windows and large, low rooms papered in plain colours. They took possession on 1 May. Ransome camped in the garden on 2 May, and Edward Thomas joined him the next day. Ivy came a fortnight later, and finally, again a fortnight later, they were joined by Tabitha and the Jamaican nanny. The nanny lasted only a fortnight. Ivy and Tabitha would stay there for the next seventeen and a half years; it was Arthur's home for little more than two of those.

It was a romantic house, snugly tucked in a crook of a hill once topped by William Beckford's great folly Fonthill Abbey, overlooking the woods of Wardour and the Wiltshire Downs, and a quarter of a mile from the Nadder, an excellent fishing river. Ransome made himself a sloping desk at which he could sit or

The Ransomes' first real home:
Manor Farm, Hatch, near
Tisbury, Wiltshire

stand (he was now suffering from piles as well as an incipient ulcer). He also had a square table covered with a baize cloth at which he sat to read books by candlelight, with his back to the fire. The fireplace was whitewashed, and around it hung his ever-growing collection of pipes. There was a door into the garden, where he could pace about and smoke under the lilac tree. They kept chickens, and bicycled around the country lanes.

All his life, Arthur found it difficult to sit still for long. He needed to pace up and down between bursts of literary inspiration, or to go for a long walk. Within a week of Tabitha's arrival at Manor Farm, he set off by train to Dauntsey, near Chippenham, and then on foot, with a tent strapped to his rucksack, for a 50-mile walk to Ryton, in Gloucestershire, home of Lascelles Abercrombie. 'It was the last of my long walks. I did some damage to my inside . . . and arrived in a very poor way indeed.' It did not stop him returning with Lascelles by train to Wincanton, and then walking the remaining 20 miles through Mere and Hinton to Hatch. A few days later, he celebrated the coronation of George V by taking part in a hard-fought village tug-of-war.

His literary energy was equally boundless. By the middle of July 1911, he had written 200 pages of the Wilde book (with frequent trips away to London and Paris for research), and was tapping out essays and reviews for the *Bookman*, the *Fortnightly Review*, the *Oxford and Cambridge Review* and a new weekly called *Eye-Witness*; he was also reading for publishers at two guineas a time.

Home life was much less satisfactory. Ivy had an exaggerated sense of her own attractions and deserts, and a bad habit learnt from her mother of getting her way by a heady mix of tantrums, manipulation and subterfuge. With the advent of a pram in the hall, Ransome was soon ruefully recalling a letter he had received just before he met Ivy from Hugh Walpole about how much of a handicap marriage was to a novelist. At the time he had shuddered at Walpole's over-effusive offer of friendship; it may even have accelerated his tumble into matrimony. Appearances were at first

maintained when Dora Collingwood came to stay for a fortnight in February 1912. She wrote in her diary:

> My godchild is charming and I am getting to like her mother very much. It is a quaint and unconventional household. There is one maid, and Ivy does a lot of the housework, and I help as much as I can. Arthur has a little book-lined study next to the sitting-room, in which I am trying to paint his portrait, but he has very little time for sittings. We have breakfast usually at 10.30 or 11, and lunch about 2, tea somewhere between 4 and 6, supper at 9. Then Ivy and Arthur play chess, and then we talk, and bed any time up until 12. It is very quiet and out of this world.

After a few days, the tone of her diary entries changes. 'I don't quite understand [Ivy] yet – she seems to be several entirely different people at different times. But she is obviously devoted to Arthur . . . and I like her for that.' Ivy lost no time in boasting that Arthur had proposed to her within half an hour of meeting her; no doubt she knew they had been rivals. Dora was soon weary of 'marvellous tales' of her earlier conquests. 'I have not seen much of Arthur,' she wrote ruefully. 'I shall be glad to get away from a household where people live on their emotions to such an extent.' Dora's visit increased Ransome's painful awareness of how different life at Hatch was from the studious calm of Lanehead.

The year 1912 was an *annus horribilis*, during which Ransome wrote with demonic energy to scant effect. 'With the quicksands of my marriage under my feet and a most unsavoury law-case ahead of me, there was nothing to be done but work.' The law case involved his *Oscar Wilde*, which had come out to critical acclaim when it was published in February 1912. A month later, he and Secker, together with the printers and the Times Book Club, were served with a joint writ for libel by Lord Alfred

RIGHT Ransome's
critical study of *Oscar
Wilde* (1912)
BELOW Ivar Campbell
(left) with Ransome and
Tabitha in the donkey
cart acquired in the
Caledonian Market

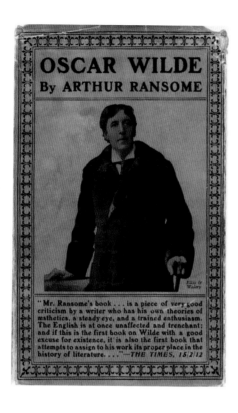

OSCAR WILDE
By ARTHUR RANSOME

"Mr. Ransome's book . . . is a piece of very good
criticism by a writer who has his own theories of
aesthetics, a steady eye, and a trained enthusiasm.
The English is at once unaffected and trenchant;
and if this is the first book on Wilde with a good
excuse for existence, it is also the first book that
attempts to assign to his work its proper place in the
history of literature. . . . "—THE TIMES, 15/2/12

Another displacement activity was breeding mice, something that
Arthur had enjoyed ever since he was a boy. A whole room, reputed
to have been the monastic privy, was given over to their cages.
The Ransomes showed them competitively, and prize certificates
adorned the walls of the 'Mouse House'. Ransome wrote a double-
page spread about breeding mice in *New Witness* (12 December
1912), and proposed a book about them to Methuen.

The marriage was becoming increasingly rocky. Ivy was neither
the first nor the last woman to find life with a dedicated writer
difficult; nor was hers the personality of a mother to the muse.
A beautiful woman and an only child, she was used to constant
admiration. At one point she claimed that she was having an affair
with Ivar Campbell, but denied it when Arthur eagerly suggested
a divorce. But Ransome too was to blame. Lounging around
reading heavyweight philosophers such as Paracelsus, Kant and
Nietzsche, tramping up hill and down dale, and smoking pipes
with congenial friends in country inns ignored the needs of a
young mother with a small baby. Dedicating the abstruse *Portraits*

Douglas. Ransome had skirted around Wilde's homosexuality,
but, after reading the uncut manuscript of *De Profundis* sent to
him by Wilde's executor Robbie Ross, he had criticized Douglas
(without naming him) for abandoning Wilde in adversity. The
ageing Douglas was notoriously litigious; he also hated Ross, to
whom Ransome's book was dedicated. Fortunately Ross backed
Ransome to the hilt, and paid the renowned lawyer Sir George
Lewis to handle the case. But Douglas refused to settle out of
court, and the trial was not to take place until a year later.

To distract himself from it, Arthur bought a donkey and a
green cart painted with yellow roses in the Caledonian Market.
He and his friend Ivar Campbell, a nephew of the Duke of Argyll,
took ten days to reach Hatch in it. 'We carried a tent and cooking
things on the cart, and a knapsack full of books for review.' Once
home, they used it for picnics and fishing trips with Tabitha, who
proudly rode on Campbell's shoulders and called him her 'Camel'.

and Speculations: An Essay in Comprehension to her did not help. His strange fable 'The Footways of Dream', also written that year and also dedicated to Ivy, is revealing. It is the story of an intensely narcissistic relationship between a man and a woman that does not survive the advent of a child: 'It may be that the footways of dream are like slender bridges, that will bear two in safety but cannot carry three.'

At around this time he and Ivy moved into separate bedrooms. Arthur explained to Tabitha that now she was big enough to get out of her cot, it was her job 'to keep Mum-Mum warm'. It is to the credit of both parents that throughout the ups and downs of her early years, Tabitha retained the feeling of being deeply loved by both her father and her mother in her early childhood.

When the Wilde case came to court in April 1913, Ivy left Tabitha with her nurse and Mrs Walker so that she could attend all four days of the hearing, embarrassing both the judge and Arthur intensely, given the then shocking aspects of Wilde's life. She was the only woman there. The case was decided in Ransome's favour, with costs awarded against Douglas. Ransome's *Wilde* became a bestseller. Ivy glowed in front of the clicking shutters of the newspaper cameras. She must have been deeply shaken when Arthur almost immediately asked her to meet Sir George Lewis to discuss a divorce. Predictably for a wife in that day and age, she flatly refused to consider it.

A few weeks later, there was a terrible scene at Hatch, which ended with her smashing two oil lamps and beating them to pieces, narrowly avoiding burning the house down. Exhausted and disgusted by both the trial and Ivy's behaviour, Ransome consulted Lewis again. 'He agreed that it was unwise to remain in the house, as in another such scene she might, without meaning it, go a little further.' Leaving Lewis to try to arrange a peaceable separation, Arthur decided to get as far away as he could, not least because he knew how deeply his nearest and dearest would disapprove of his decision to leave Ivy. He acquired a passport,

A playful Ivy in the garden at Hatch

and headed for the most exciting and inaccessible place he could possibly have chosen: Russia. It was an ideal 'stepping-stone to escape' because not only was it more than 1,300 miles from Wiltshire, but it required a passport, so that Ivy would be unable to chase after him, as she had done when he went to Paris. It meant leaving Tabitha, his adored daughter, but he decided that 'anything would be better than for my daughter to grow up as her mother had grown up, forever playing her father off against her mother, her mother against her father'.

FOREIGN AFFAIRS
(1913–24)

YOUNG ARTHUR'S RUSSIAN TALES

'Moscow! Like a flash the Russia of Seton Merriman – the only Russia I knew – passed before my eyes. Adventure, danger, romance photographed themselves in my mind.'
Bruce Lockhart, on being sent to Russia by the Foreign Office in 1912, Memoirs of a British Agent, *1933*

The parts of Arthur Ransome's autobiography that deal with his many assignments as a foreign correspondent in Russia, Finland, the Baltic States, Rumania, Germany, Egypt, the Sudan and China show him as Captain Flint incarnate. Put together, they would be the memoir Uncle Jim is struggling to write in *Swallows and Amazons*: 'Mixed Moss: The Story of a Rolling Stone'. Ransome's eleven years in Eastern Europe were hectic and productive: he wrote over seven hundred lengthy and detailed reports for the *Daily News* and the *Manchester Guardian*, five books and several pamphlets.

No one has established exactly when or why Ransome became deeply interested in Russia. Like Lockhart, he would have read Seton Merriman's thrilling novel *The Sowers* (1895), in which a compassionate Russian prince tries to relieve the sufferings of the peasants, only to find himself a hunted pariah. He had met the influential Russian critic Dmitri Sergeyevich Merezhkovsky (1865–1941) in Paris, where all things Russian were the rage.

After the Russian ballet had arrived in London in 1911, interest burgeoned in England as well. Several travel books were published in 1912, as was Post Wheeler's *Russian Wonder Tales*. In the London Library Ransome read Ralston's *Russian Folk Tales*. He was sure that he could do better than either if he went to Russia and learnt the language.

He consulted Bernard Pares, head of the newly established School of Russian Studies at Liverpool, about going to Russia to study folklore, and visited his mother in Edinburgh to explain that he needed to escape. Late in May 1913, he boarded a cargo boat for Copenhagen. He intended to go much further. Ralph Courtney, who was married to the daughter of the Spanish Consul in St Petersburg, had given him an introduction to the Gellibrands, an Anglo-Russian family who owned a timber company in St Petersburg.

Being on board ship worked an instant magic. The smell of lilac and the sight of Elsinore Castle in the early morning mist brought Hans Christian Andersen to mind. From Copenhagen Ransome took a ferry to Malmo, then a train to Stockholm, then

Ransome in the sheepskin hat and thick military overcoat that protected him from the Moscow winter of 1915

ABOVE Ivy sightseeing at Arles in June 1914

OPPOSITE Ransome playing chequers with a young Russian, c.1915

a steamer to St Petersburg. Edmund Gellibrand met him on the quay, and they went straight to his country estate in Terioki, on the shore of the Gulf of Finland some 30 miles north-west of St Petersburg. For four blissful months, Ransome read and wrote, walked, swam and fished.

Friends and relations were shocked by his exodus. Edith stood by him, for all her doubts. Ransome immersed himself in the Russian language, beginning with children's primers and graduating to reading whole newspapers with the aid of a dictionary. He got to know St Petersburg and made a host of friends. Domestically, he could not have been more comfortable: the hospitable Anglo-Russian families who lived in St Petersburg's luxurious English Quarter were among the wealthiest of its inhabitants. He sent a steady stream of articles back to England, some about Russia, some translations of folk tales.

After nearly four months away, Arthur returned to England via Riga, Berlin and Paris (where his *Wilde* was being translated),

arriving at the end of September 1913. He went to Leeds to see his mother and sisters, and to Lanehead to visit the Collingwoods. Then he returned to Hatch to give the marriage another chance. He stayed for six months, which were punctuated by visits to friends and relations. Tabitha was now three and a half, an enchanting age. There were more fishing expeditions. Tabitha later remembered 'Dor-Dor' coming back soaked and bathing in a slipper bath in front of the fire, smoking a pipe and holding his legs out one at a time to be sponged by Ivy. Following in his grandfather Tom Ransome's footsteps, Arthur interested himself in photography, setting up a darkroom.

In March 1914, the Ransomes had another fortnight in Paris, leaving Tabitha with Edith. Word had reached Arthur of a job there that would justify a return to Russia. Nothing came of it, but he did get a commission to write an English guide to St Petersburg for the visitors who were going there in ever-increasing numbers. He planned to write it in a month, and then go on with his folk tales. The price of Arthur's return to Russia was for Ivy to join him in St Petersburg when he had found a suitable flat. In the event, Ivy decided not to go to Russia; instead she left Tabitha with Edith and toured southern France with friends; in June she was in Monte Carlo.

Ransome finished the guidebook on 9 July, just twelve days after Archduke Ferdinand of Austria was shot dead by a Serb nationalist. Feeling 'thunder in the air', but unaware how dramatically the tectonic plates of European diplomacy were about to shift, he took a train from St Petersburg to join the Gellibrands at their summer home at Terioki. A month later news of Austria's ultimatum to Serbia and of Russia's mobilization in support of the Serbs reached them. With a sense of unreality, he watched the streets fill with conscripts. Strikes and unrest were forgotten: the new soldiers lined up to be blessed by Tsar Nicholas. In August 1914, Ransome wrote to Dorrie:

The tennis court where I was playing a month ago is a cavalry camp. The streets are full of soldiers. And, well, I always admired the Russians, but never so much as now. You know how our soldiers go off in pomp with flags and music. I have not heard a note of music since the declaration of war. They go off quite silently here in the middle of the night, carrying their little tin kettles, and for all the world like puzzled children going off to school for the first time. And the idea in all their heads is fine. They all say the same thing. 'We hate fighting. But if we can stop Germany then there will be peace for ever.'

Germany declared war on Russia on 1 August, and on France on 3 August, and then swept through Belgium on 4 August. To Russia's delight, England promptly declared war on Germany. Volunteers surged forward; within a month the British army had tripled in size from 220,000 to three-quarters of a million. Ransome set off for England on 18 August. In a voyage reminiscent of Erskine Childers' prescient thriller *Riddle of the Sands*, his ship dodged the Germans' Baltic fleet to reach first Stockholm and then Oslo. From there he took ship for Hull, skirting minefields on the Northumbrian coast. He went straight to Hatch, where he wrote several articles about what he had witnessed in Russia, and his experiences afterwards. Like the rest of the world, he had no idea that the conflict would drag on for four whole years, but he rightly concluded that, win or lose, Russia's traditional imperial absolutism was doomed because the war effort relied on the support of the reformists. Where he was wrong was in predicting a golden age of Russian constitutional monarchy.

For the next four months he was based at Hatch writing articles and folk tales and fishing. He caught up with friends and relatives, spending several weeks with the Collingwoods at Lanehead. More than anything, he agonized about the war. Among the hundreds of thousands of volunteers responding to Kitchener's 'Your Country Needs You' was Geoffrey Ransome. Should Arthur join up too? He was extremely short-sighted, and suffered from unpredictable bouts of stomach troubles, migraines and piles; now thirty years old, he was also at the top end of the age for enlistment. Friends (Harold Williams, Bernard Pares and, most influentially of all, his godfather's son Francis Acland, now Permanent Under-Secretary of State for Foreign Affairs) were all of the same mind: he would be of far more use putting his now extensive Russian connections to use as a reporter on the unpredictable situation in Russia.

Ransome entertained hopes of being made a King's Messenger, but these privileged posts were usually held by army personnel. Acland may already have been planning for him to be useful in a less official capacity. He persuaded a publisher to commission a history of Russia from Ransome, so that he had a respectable cover story. In addition, Arthur had a commission for his book of folk tales. He left for Russia again just before Christmas, giving Ivy a fishing rod as a present. It was the last prolonged visit he would make to Hatch. He returned to Britain for six weeks late in 1915, one month (November) in 1916 and two (17 October–21 December) in 1917, visiting Hatch but not staying for very long. He and Ivy seem to have established some kind of *modus vivendi* on these brief visits. Ransome records 'amicable angling with Ivy' and 'quiet fishing in Wiltshire' in November 1915; 'fishing in Wiltshire' in September 1916 and catching a perch in October 1917. Ivy hoped that after the war was over, Arthur would come back to her. 'She still has an irreducible maximum of admiration and affection for him,' wrote Edward Thomas, after a visit to Hatch in 1915. 'The place is very full of him, his pipes and books, photographs of him, certificates of prizes which his white mice have won, etc.'

OUR MAN IN PETROGRAD

'I love Russia more and more . . . I know no place in the world except Coniston or Cartmel
where I get the same gorgeous feeling of freedom and living with the whole of oneself.
I am now able to talk to anybody, and understand pretty well everything,
and I don't know which I like better, the people or the country.'

Arthur Ransome, letter to Edith Ransome, 1915

Ransome landed in Norway on Christmas Day 1914, and reached Petrograd on New Year's Eve. Harold Williams welcomed him warmly, posting him off to Moscow to get a wider picture of what was going on. Although his lodgings were alive with cockroaches, Arthur revelled in exploring the ancient city, despite the snow and ice clinging to his moustache and spectacles. One of the first people he met was Hugh Walpole, who, like him, had agonized over joining up, knowing that he was utterly useless without glasses, but had landed a job as Russian correspondent for the *Daily Mail*, despite having no Russian. Ransome bought a warm overcoat and a fishing rod, and explored Moscow thoroughly for a couple of months. He worked on an update of his guide to

LEFT View from the lodgings which Ransome took in Glinka Street, St Petersburg, in 1916
RIGHT Ransome's much-stamped passport from his years in Russia

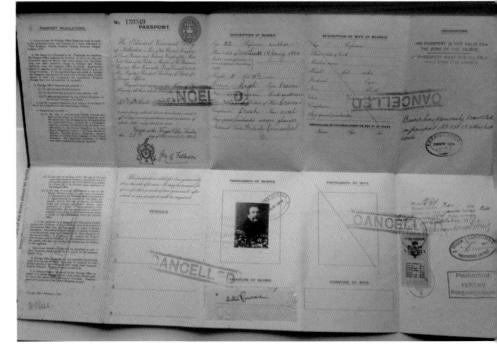

THE WORLD OF ARTHUR RANSOME

St Petersburg called *From Petersburg to Petrograd* and on the book of folk tales that would eventually appear as *Old Peter's Russian Tales*, and saw Walpole nearly every day. A prolific novelist, Walpole was working on a book set in Russia. Before he left for Petrograd, he gave Ransome some practical tips: use a loose-leaf notebook, head the first page 'Chapter 1', and get going.

Arthur never mastered Walpole's facility, but he was sufficiently inspired to write *The Elixir of Life*, a dashing romance about a necromancer. It was published by Methuen in May 1915, not at all the right time for such light-hearted escapism, and sank like a stone. Ransome was disappointed but had worse things on his mind. He was suffering acutely from haemorrhoids, losing quantities of 'gore'. His friends the Williams sent him to stay

OPPOSITE When he could, Arthur went fishing in Russian lakes and rivers

ABOVE LEFT Picnicking with Hugh Walpole in the Russian woods
ABOVE RIGHT 1938 dust jacket of *Old Peter's Russian Tales* (first published 1916), using decorations by the book's illustrator, Dimitry Mitrokhin

with friends of theirs at Vergheza, on the River Volkhov, near Novgorod, and there his health improved somewhat; best of all he got the peace and support that enabled him to finish his book of Russian folk tales.

Old Peter's Russian Tales was an important milestone in his literary progress. The stories were written as if told aloud around a fireside. Although he dedicated it to Barbara Collingwood, its introduction shows that he also had Tabitha, and the Lake Country, in mind. 'This is a book written far away in Russia, for English children who play in deep lanes with wild roses above them in the high hedges, or by the small singing brooks that dance down the grey fells at home.' Published in 1916, it has been enjoyed (and shivered over) by generations of children, and is still in print today.

In October, he made a whistle-stop tour of England, visiting his mother and Geoffrey, who had been injured, and spending a week at Hatch and a few days at Lanehead. He was back in Petrograd by 3 November, and in February 1916 he settled into

FAR LEFT Lola Kinel, whose account of meeting Ransome in 1916 appears in her autobiography *Under Five Eagles* (1937)
LEFT Ransome in the Press Corps uniform which he wore when visiting the Eastern Front in 1916. His cap is initialled AK; his name, Russian-style, was Artur Kirrilovich (Arthur, son of Cyril)

OPPOSITE This illustration by Dimitry Mitrokhin of the burning of Litovsky Castle in 1916 was commissioned by Ransome for the book he planned to write on the Russian Revolution

attractive new quarters in Glinka Street, in the very heart of the city. From there he looked out on the cataclysmic events of the next few years as if from the bridge of a ship.

Although wary of emotional entanglements during his first few years in Russia, he continued to enjoy female company. In *Under Five Eagles,* the Polish writer Lola Kinel writes of meeting him on a Finnish train. 'He was tall, dressed in a Russian military coat, though without any insignia, and a fur cap. He had long red moustaches, completely concealing his mouth and humorous, twinkling eyes.' She was playing chess, and 'in delightful, broken Russian' he asked if he could come in and watch. Soon he was playing. Lola told him that she was hoping to get a job in Petrograd, and when they parted, he gave her his card. On it, printed in Russian, was 'Artur Kirrilovich [son of Cyril] Ransom [sic], correspondent *Daily News*', with below it, in tiny English letters, 'Arthur Ransome'. She got in

touch, and since she was an excellent linguist, Arthur gave her a job: skimming Petrograd's thirty or more daily newspapers every morning in search of news that might be of interest in England and translating it. Her description of his huge room in Glinka Street shows how completely he had reverted to his happy Bohemian existence in Chelsea.

It was the first bachelor room I had ever seen: it had a desk and typewriter in one corner; in another a bed, night table, and dresser, all behind a screen; then a sort of social arrangement consisting of an old sofa and a round table with some chairs round it, in the centre. And *books*. They were everywhere, heaped in rows on old dressers, heaped on chairs, heaped on the sofa and even on the floor. Among these books I found occasionally torn, soiled socks. I used to pick them up gingerly, with my gloved hand, and wrap them in a piece of newspaper.

'Doesn't anyone ever mend your socks for you?' I asked one day.

'No. Don't bother picking those up. I wear them, and throw them away when they get torn. The maid forgot to take these away.'

'But then you must buy an awful lot of socks.'

'I do. These Russian *prachki* (laundresses) never bother to mend things. I live like a wild rabbit.'

'And look at your desk – look at all this dust. Doesn't the maid ever dust here?'

'I would wring her neck if she did. She daren't touch my desk,' he said with the air of a fanatic threatened with some danger.

In the middle of March, Lenin arrived in Petrograd and there were violent confrontations between the Bolsheviks and the police all over the city. Kinel recalled the exhilaration of the early days of revolution. 'The feeling of witnessing something very grand, something tremendous . . . helped one, too, in disregarding danger . . . I had the conviction that I – Lola Kinel – was entirely immune from bullets and death.' Ransome was a better judge of peril. When Lola refused to retreat when she and 'AK' were caught in crossfire between revolutionaries and Tsarist troops, 'he raised me in his arms and began to run'.

Lola recalls that Ransome was much more enthusiastic about Bolshevism than she was, and describes his fury when she accused him of being too romantic, and warned him that neither of them knew enough to judge. He accused her in turn of selfishness: 'The revolution needs people like you, young, intelligent people.' Rather in love with him, she tried to make up their quarrel by arriving with a poem, but 'AK', perhaps cautious, remained aloof.

In the autumn, Ransome returned to England, completely

missing the Russian Revolution of October 1917. He came back to turmoil. He saw the revolutionaries march past singing the Marseillaise and waving red flags, and flames leaping from the notorious Litovsky Castle prison. Shortly afterwards, he removed to Moscow. He and Lola next met when he paid Petrograd a flying visit in the spring of 1918. He asked her to buy him a long list of books because he did not have time to scour the bookshops. She wondered if he was planning a Conradesque historical romance when she saw such titles as *The Mexican Rebellion*, *Partisan War*, *Guerrilla Warfare* and *Tactics*. In fact, she was disconcerted to discover when she triumphantly delivered them to Ransome that they were for Trotsky. 'He is building a Red Army, you know, and, not being a soldier, he doesn't know much about it,' he told her. 'So he is trying to learn all about it from books.' Ransome had another reason for helping Trotsky: he was keen to impress a strapping young woman called Evgenia Shelepina.

AMAZON INCARNATE

'My principal friends here are Radek and his wife, and two huge young women, Bolsheviks,
as tall as Grenadiers, who prefer pistols to powder puffs, and swords to parasols.'
Arthur Ransome, letter to Edith Ransome, 21 May 1918

She was scraping burnt potatoes out of a coffee pot, and reproaching the vodka-sodden censor for not attending more carefully to his surreptitious meal, on the first occasion that Arthur met her. As tall as he was and healthily brawny, this forceful, pipe-smoking girl was an unlikely match for a man who had hitherto fallen for petite women like Pixie Coleman-Smith, the Collingwood girls, Jessie Gavin and Ivy, whom he could fondly liken to fairies. Saving the potatoes and ticking off the censor were entirely in character. Such competence had brought Evgenia Petrovna Shelepina to

Front portico of the 'vast and labyrinthine' Smolny Institute, in which Ransome first courted Evgenia Shelepina

the notice of Lev Trotsky, the Bolshevik 'Commissar for Foreign Affairs', whose private secretary she then was. Ransome had seen her the day before among Trotsky's entourage, 'a tall jolly girl', who had taken notes when he interviewed Trotsky on 31 December 1917. When he returned to the vast and labyrinthine Smolny Institute the next day in search of the censor's stamp for his latest despatch, she had been chatting to her sister, who worked in the typing pool. She had known just where the censor was, and once she had bullied the tired old man into stamping the despatch, she invited Arthur back for tea after he had posted it. He accepted.

Evgenia was twenty-three, ten years younger than Arthur. Her father had been curator of the imperial palace gardens, and time would show that she inherited his passion for plants. The American correspondent Edgar Sissons recalled that 'her tiny feet was the big girl's pride', and that she wore expensive high-heeled shoes despite the deep and uneven ice and snow in the city streets. Over the next few months, Ransome saw a great deal of Evgenia, her sister Eroida, her friend Rosa and Rosa's husband Karl Radek, the exuberant and elegant head of the Press Bureau at the Commissariat. In a capitalized letter to Tabitha, he described her as 'A BIG GIRL AS BIG AS DORDOR WHO CARRIES A REVOLVER AND A SWORD AND IS A FIERCE REVOLUTIONARY'. Ransome admired Radek, describing him as 'spectacled, revolutionary goblin of incredible intelligence and vivacity'. He swallowed his party line like a gullible trout, regurgitating it in what was on occasion appalling hyperbole. 'I walk these abominable, unswept, mountainously dirt-clogged, snow-clogged streets in exaltation. It is like walking

Russian studio photographs (undated) of Evgenia and Arthur

on Wetherlam or Dow Crag, with the future of mankind spreading before one like the foothills of the Lake Country, and the blue seas to the West,' ran one particularly purple passage written in late January, 1918.

London disapproved of Ransome's opinion that the Bolsheviks were bound to prevail in Russia, and his reports were squeezed out of the papers almost completely. In May 1918, Ransome's *On Behalf of Russia: An Open Letter to the American People* was published. Towards the end of the month, he wrote to Ivy asking for a divorce. She refused. So, goes Evgenia's memoir, 'after a lot of heart and conscience searching we decided that as we could not marry we shall live together without being legally married'.

By June, the Bolshevik cause seemed all but lost. The British had occupied Murmansk, and Anglo-Russian relations had deteriorated so badly that Ransome decided that he should leave Russia. Lockhart persuaded the Foreign Office to let Ransome put Evgenia on his passport, but in the event they decided it would be safer to travel separately. Arthur left Petrograd as an Englishman, and then donned the uniform of a Bolshevik courier to travel through German-occupied Finland. In his despatch case were three million roubles, proof positive to the Bolshevik Legation in Stockholm that he was a bona fide friend.

Evgenia accompanied Vorovsky, head of the Legation, who was travelling via Germany. She arrived on 28 August, and a few days later they went for a sail in a small oak-built cutter with a member of the Legation, hoping that it might be suitable for them to live on while they were in Sweden. However, it was pronounced too small, and instead they set up house in a cottage on the shore, looking out at the scattered islands of the Stockholm archipelago.

Russia, meanwhile, was in turmoil. Violent demonstrations by breakaway socialist groups culminated in the attempted assassination of Lenin by Dora Kaplan on 30 August, and 500 hostages were shot in the consequent backlash of 'Red Terror'.

Moscow

The official boot

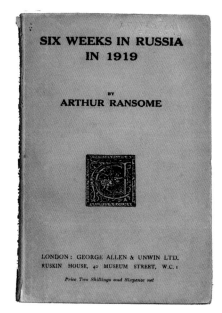

SIX WEEKS IN RUSSIA
IN 1919

BY
ARTHUR RANSOME

LONDON: GEORGE ALLEN & UNWIN LTD.
RUSKIN HOUSE, 40 MUSEUM STREET, W.C. 1
Price Two Shillings and Sixpence net

The British Embassy in Petrograd was sacked and the naval attaché Captain Crombie was murdered. In America there were outcries at Ransome's persistence in supporting the Bolsheviks, but in Britain his argument that he was better placed to provide 'knowledge rather than news' than any other journalist in Russia was accepted. Early in October he was approached by Clifford Sharp of the SIS, and enrolled as S76.

On 11 November 1918, the much-longed-for Armistice was signed, but Britain remained at war with Soviet Russia, and put pressure on Sweden to expel the Bolshevik Legation. They expelled Ransome as well. 'Slightly bald; hair parted on the left; narrow, shrewd eyes; large, bushy moustache; wears pince-nez' ran the official description of him. Aware that he was uniquely well placed to pass on intelligence, he decided to return to Moscow with the Legation rather than return to England. Sharp approved, assuring the London office that 'S76 may be regarded as absolutely honest. If you ask him any question about any of his numerous activities in Russia, you will get the exact truth. His reports about the conditions in Russia may also be relied upon absolutely with

only the proviso that his views tend to be coloured by his personal sympathies with men like Litvinov and Radek. He will report what he sees but he does not see quite straight.'

Back in Moscow in January 1919, Ransome collected material, including several interviews with Lenin and other revolutionary leaders. In March, he returned to England, and was arrested on arrival because of his supposed Bolshevik sympathies. However, the Foreign Office stood by him, and he was rapidly freed. He then set to work to write *Six Weeks in Russia in 1919*, which created huge interest when it was published in June.

His problem now was the extraction of Evgenia. Fortunately the success of *Six Weeks* led C. P. Scott, editor of the *Manchester Guardian*, to invite him to be the paper's Russian correspondent for six months. By 22 October, Arthur arrived in Moscow via Estonia, celebrating his reunion with Evgenia by introducing her to Horlicks Milk Tablets. He also brought with him messages to Lenin from the Estonian government. He and Evgenia set off on 28 October, arriving in Reval, Estonia, on 5 November. This time, Ransome was carrying a peace proposal from Lenin to the

FAR LEFT 'The official boot': Ransome's cartoon of his ejection from Stockholm, from a letter written to his mother in November 1918

LEFT In *Six Weeks in Russia* in 1919, 'a bald record of things done and things seen', Ransome praised 'the extraordinary vitality' of the revolution

RIGHT Two sides of Evgenia: (above) befurred and glamorous and (below) a doughty ship's mate

Estonians, an act of derring-do that he would later claim was his greatest political achievement. Recently discovered Russian records suggest that Evgenia was also acting as a courier, carrying with her a packet full of diamonds and pearls worth over a million roubles destined for the Bolshevik cause. Was this the price of her freedom, as it had been of Ransome's when he escaped to Stockholm in June 1918, or part of the Estonian deal? The wording of the letter that he typed for her to sign soon after they arrived suggests, however, that the discovery was a shock to him.

> Dear Arthur, I hereby promise you on my word of
> honour that I will undertake no political commissions
> in England from the Bolsheviks or any other political
> party, and further that I will engage in no conspiratorial
> work whatsoever without expressly informing you that
> I consider this promise no longer binding.

Evgenia honoured her promise. When she did finally reach England as Arthur's wife, she always refused to discuss the years in Russia, and remained suspicious of strangers for many years; given the vengeful attacks of Stalin's agents on Trotsky and his followers, she may just have had good cause.

THE MAKING OF A SAILOR

*'I have got so accustomed to writing on board that I may not be able
to put a sentence together in a room that does not rock just a little.'*
Arthur Ransome, letter to Edith Ransome, 2 October 1922

Although the Lake Country was always Ransome's primary spiritual home, he had a secondary vision of paradise: living on board boats. Learning to sail *Swallow*, *Toob* and *Jamrach*, and taking the occasional fishing holiday on the Broads, had whetted his appetite for greater things: cabin yachts. There is some evidence that Ransome owned a little yacht himself as early as 1916. He seems to have quietly bought her in a Solent boatyard on one of his visits to England, perhaps for a song because she was in need of TLC. She is mentioned in an upbeat finale to an otherwise miserable letter that he wrote to his mother on 26 February 1917.

Some day or other, regardless of the advantages of a settled income, I shall fling my typewriter over the moon, catch it with a joyful yell on the other side, and spend three years on pouring out novels – at least romances – in collaboration with Joyce, and a mass of fairy stories in collaboration with myself. We will live on a farm. We will live on my boat. Said yacht meanwhile is decaying away, and will be in an awful state when the war is over. Still, I daresay with plenty of candle grease in the worst leaks she'll float in still water and allow me to sit in the cabin and hammer out books worth writing.

When his mother told him in late 1918 that she was renting a house in West Malling, near Rochester in Kent, he wrote, 'I shall bring my yacht round from Southampton . . . there is a lovely harbour at Ramsgate. My boat must have some sort of harbour to lie in, she being too big and deep-keeled to be beached.' Nothing more is known of what sounds like a capacious vessel, so presumably she was beyond repair when he returned to England for good in 1924.

The tumultuous events in Russia had made any kind of boating, except to fish, impossible for the last five years. But in December 1919, Arthur and Evgenia found lodgings 40 miles

If not, why not? Read him at once, and then you will have a happy New Year

Goodbye for now

This is a young Cockyollybird, reading *Robinson Crusoe*. Observe her contented expression

LEFT Detail showing *Slug* from a December 1918 letter from Arthur to Tabitha west of Reval in a wooden house in the forest at the head of Lahepe Bay. There Ransome had a quiet writing room and no domestic responsibilities. Now that the war was over, he was free of the treadmill of the *Daily News* telegrams. He settled down to learn Estonian, research Baltic history and write articles for the *Manchester Guardian*. 'I'm immensely interested in this democratic little republic,' he wrote to his mother. 'It seems to me possibly a sample in miniature of the sort of thing which Russia itself will develop if only we have the sense to stop trying at great expense to turn her into a reactionary.'

From his balcony enticing islands were visible at the mouth of the bay, and steamers and sailing boats large and small could be seen heading west to Riga, north to Helsingfors and east to Reval. At last he could indulge his longing to sail, perhaps even live aboard. His first boat was a clumsy green 18-footer with no cabin, which a Reval fisherman sold him in June 1920 for £10. She had a short iron bowsprit, stone ballast and a gaff and staysail rig similar to those of *Jamrach* and *Swallow*. They christened her *Slug*, 'for her speed'. When he told Evgenia that he was going to sail their little ship back to Lahepe Bay, some 60 miles, she announced she was coming too, though she had never sailed before.

To undertake such a voyage suggests that Ransome had done at least a little coastal sailing in the yacht he mentioned in those letters to his mother, as well as cruising the Broads and the Swedish archipelago. They reached Lahepe safely three days later, after one night on an island and another uneasily napping on the stone ballast. Ransome began to plan a book about sailing on the Baltic, 'a jolly sort of travel book, with lots of camping and fishing and sailing shoved in', and well larded with Estonian history and folklore. By 21 January 1921, when he wrote to his mother asking her to send him E. F. Knight's *Falcon on the Baltic*,

ABOVE The Ransomes preserved *Slug*'s flag all their lives
BELOW Arthur and Evgenia in the fishing dinghy made for them in Riga in 1921

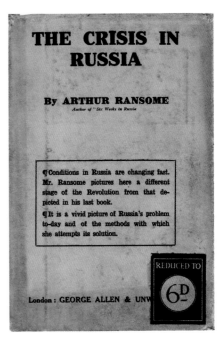

THE CRISIS IN RUSSIA

By ARTHUR RANSOME
Author of " Six Weeks in Russia"

¶ Conditions in Russia are changing fast. Mr. Ransome pictures here a different stage of the Revolution from that depicted in his last book.
¶ It is a vivid picture of Russia's problem to-day and of the methods with which she attempts its solution.

REDUCED TO **6**ᴰ

London : GEORGE ALLEN & UNW

LEFT Evgenia on *Kittywake*, punningly named after Ransome's adoptive sister, Kitty Woodburne
RIGHT Ransome's 1921 *The Crisis in Russia* reported on the dire state of the famine-struck country's economy

he had persuaded Allen & Unwin to commission it. But there was no question of voyaging far in *Slug*.

They had higher hopes of the 16-foot carvel-built yacht *Kittywake* that they bought in 1921. She had a cabin 'quite extraordinarily roomy for her diminutive size', and Evgenia made mattresses and orange curtains for the tiny portholes. On the downside, her cockpit was so small that 'one felt as if one was in the pouch of a catapult'. She was skittish and top heavy, and her bunks were too short and too narrow. They began to dream of 'a really good boat, big and comfortable to live on board for months on end and fit to be sailed to England if and when we wanted to do so'.

Between nautical experiments, Ransome was keeping his finger on the pulse of developments in Moscow, which was easily accessible from Estonia once the truce between the countries was signed in February 1920. He was given an office of his own in the Commissariat for Foreign Affairs. After a fact-finding mission for the *Manchester Guardian* to parts of the country hard-hit by the famine, he collected his published and unpublished reports to make up *The Crisis in Russia*. Published in 1921, this described the extreme hardships endured, and praised communist efficiency and determination in alleviating it. Either through ignorance or because of his own vulnerable position, Ransome remained silent on Lenin's ruthless extermination of enemies. He was certainly under surveillance. Returning via Petrograd in April 1920, he found his rooms there sacked: his priceless collection of telegrams, interviews and notes chronicling the years of the revolution was lost. Still on the books of the SIS, but not trusted by many in England and seen by Lenin as a useful mouthpiece for propaganda, he was in an unenviable position. But at least he had time to sail.

RACUNDRA'S THREE CRUISES

*'Grown-up people (if those who love sailing ever grow up, which I doubt)
are like children in taking particular pleasure in stories that tell of adventures
that might, with luck, happen to themselves.'*
Arthur Ransome, introduction to E. K. Knight's Falcon on the Baltic

Arthur and Evgenia had been fantasizing about their dream boat for over a year when they met the man who could build it. 'In evening went and fell in love with Mr Eggers, with the probable result that we shall have a boat built by him,' wrote Ransome in his diary for 15 April 1921. The charismatic Otto Eggers had once designed and built the fastest racing yachts in the Baltic, but had lost his Reval yard because he was German. Over many a pipe, he, Arthur and Evgenia planned a broad-beamed double-ender well suited to the stormy conditions of the Baltic, and indeed the North Sea. She was to be a cruising boat that one man could manage if need be, but on which three could be comfortable. The cabin was to be large enough for the strapping couple to stand up and walk around in without bumping into each other. She was to have a writing-table a full yard square, a place for a typewriter, a bookcase and broad bunks for sleep 'without bruising knee and elbow with each unconsidered movement'.

Having commissioned Eggers to draw up her blueprints, Arthur and Evgenia set off in *Kittywake* for Baltic Port, some 35 miles west. In August they moved 150 miles south to Latvia, renting a small lakeside house just outside Riga. There they found a boat builder who made them such a good little dinghy for fishing and sailing that they decided to ask him to build Eggers' boat. He said he could do so by April 1922. Evgenia swore she could do without new clothes for the next two years. Arthur 'took a deep breath and signed the contract, determined one way or another to do enough writing to pay for it . . . This was among the few wise things I have

done in my life, for, more than anything else, this boat helped me to get back to my proper trade of writing.'

That winter, they watched their ship slowly coming to life in the boatshed while ice yachts flitted effortlessly as birds across the frozen bay; Arthur told Edith about 'a fine sail' in a big one. They chatted to the old man who looked after yachts and dinghies at the club. Carl Sehmel had served on *Thermopylae*, and Lady Brassey's famous *Sunbeam*, and Ransome was delighted when he agreed to crew for them.

High summer of 1922 arrived with their dreamship still unfinished. In mid-August, Ransome lost patience with the

Racundra's plumply comfortable lines, from *Racundra's First Cruise* (1923)

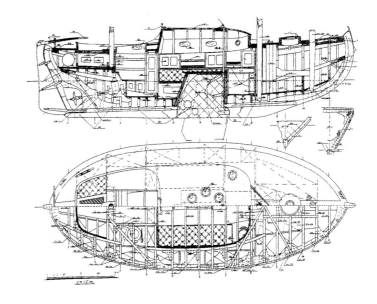

boatyard, and brought her round to the yacht club to finish fitting her out himself with the help of Sehmel. She was named *Racundra*, a word derived from Ra (Ransome), c (for Carl Sehmel), und (and) and ra (for Evgenia), soon also to be a Ransome. Remembering that *Slug*'s sails had been stolen, Arthur slept aboard until they set off on an ambitious circular cruise to Helsinki via Reval. On 20 August, he had his customary dawn dip while porridge was cooking on the primus. An hour later, Sehmel came aboard, followed a little later by Evgenia. The story of their island-hopping voyage is told in *Racundra's First Cruise*. Evgenia is tactfully disguised as 'the Cook'; Sehmel is 'the Ancient Mariner', whose red stocking-cap with a tassel put Ransome in mind of 'a gnome, a pixie or a fairy cobbler' – and eventually of an Amazon pirate.

They sailed from Riga to the romantically remote island of Runo, then to Moon, Baltic Port and Reval, then across the Gulf of Finland to Helsingfors, then back via Reval, Baltic Port and Dago to Riga. When the September equinox finally 'flung us home with a flick of his mighty tail', they had sailed over 700 miles in five weeks. Ransome had taken eighty photographs and written over 30,000 words. 'I think that when I have revised the stuff I wrote while actually sailing, and worked in the material I collected last year, I should have a pretty jolly little book,' he wrote to Edith in October 1922. Ivy had at last agreed to a divorce, and he went on to say that they were planning to sail to England in *Racundra* as soon as the divorce came through, 'so as to have a second book to follow up'.

Racundra had been laid up for the winter at the yacht club soon after their return on 26 September. Ransome had to spend

the rest of October and some of November in Moscow. He went to England in December, and discussed terms for the divorce with Ivy, and then returned to Riga to spend Christmas with Evgenia. He sent Allen & Unwin the completed manuscript on 20 January, including charts and photographs. In February, he went to Moscow again for the *Guardian*. While he was away, the house in Riga burnt down. Fortunately the cat woke Evgenia, and she escaped without injury, but all their personal possessions and the equipment they had carefully removed from *Racundra* for safety were destroyed.

Racundra's First Cruise was published in England in July 1923, and in America in November. 'The publisher guarantees a jolly time, and will refund your money if you become sea-sick. You don't need to know the difference between nautical chalk and cheese to enjoy this jolliest of yarns,' ran the blurb. Jolly it was, a wonderful mixture of perilous passage-making, Estonian history and geography, and nautical technicalities. Journalism had knocked the whimsy out of Ransome's writing: with *Racundra* he developed the straightforward way of telling how things are done that is such a winning feature

of his books for children. In an appendix, he gave a loving and minutely detailed description of *Racundra's* interior.

Encouraged by the excellent sales of the book, and the interest in sailing in Baltic waters expressed by members of the Cruising Association, Ransome decided on another cruise to provide a Baltic sequel. With them went Oureberes, a 3-foot long grass snake named (albeit mispelt) for Arthur's boyhood chum Eric Eddison's romance *The Worm Ouroboros*. 'Oureberes travels in a huge jam-jar, crawls hither and thither on deck and over the cabin table and is happiest curled round and round the bottom of a teapot,' Arthur recorded in his diary-log. Sehmel family legend has it that at night Oureberes was happiest curled around Evgenia's breasts. They set off for Petrograd from Riga on 18 July, and reached Reval six days later.

In Reval, Ransome received a summons from Ivy's solicitors asking him to return to England for an urgent meeting. The divorce negotiations were at last under way. It was mid-August by the time he got back, so there was time only to cruise to Finland, which Evgenia had not seen in the first cruise, as she had opted to stay in Reval for

'Not only can one stand up in *Racundra*'s cabin, but one can walk about there, and that without interfering with anyone who may be sitting at the writing-table, which is a yard square . . . The bunks are wider than is usual, yet behind and above each bunk are two deep cupboards, with between them a deep open space divided by a shelf, used on the port side for books and on the starboard side for crockery . . . *Racundra* was designed as a boat in which it would be possible to work, and, as a floating study or office, I think it would be hard to improve upon her. The writing-table is forward of the port bunk, and a Lettish workman made me an admirable little three-legged stool, which, when the ship is underway, stows under the table. Above and behind the ample field of the table is a deep cupboard and a bookcase, of a height to take the Nautical Almanac, the Admiralty Pilot, Dixon Kemp and Norie's invaluable Epitome and Tables. Under the shelf for nautical books is a shallow drawer where I keep a set of pocket tools, nails, screws and such things. Under the writing-table is a big chart drawer, where I keep the charts immediately in use, writing and drawing materials, parallel rulers, protractors, surveying compass, stop-watch and other small gear. By the side of this is a long narrow drawer, used for odds and ends, and underneath that is a special cupboard made to take my portable typewriter.'

Arthur Ransome, *Racundra's First Cruise*

ABOVE Evgenia's grass snake Oureberes accompanied her on *Racundra*'s second cruise, in July 1923
RIGHT *Racundra* in a quiet creek during her third cruise, in August 1924

OPPOSITE Evgenia and Arthur brewing up in the Baltic

THE WORLD OF ARTHUR RANSOME

that leg of the voyage. Wirgo, ex-British Consul in Estonia, came with them. Although they had one glorious night and day of sailing, they were gale-bound in Helsingfors for several days, and buffeted by wind and rain for most of the time. Ransome's autobiography blanks out the dispirited end to this interrupted voyage.

He returned to Moscow to report on reactions to the controversial and aggressive ultimatum offered in May 1923 by Curzon, the British Foreign Secretary, then returned to England for October and November. In December, he went to Moscow again to interview Iury Libedinsky, whose novel *A Week* he had just translated into English. He arrived back in Riga to spend Christmas Day with Evgenia, but had to go to Moscow again in January to report on the death of Lenin and repercussions from it. On 2 February, Ransome's deeply unpopular recommendation that the British recognize the Soviet government was acted upon. Interventionism ended. Ransome returned to England and finalized his divorce on 8 April 1924, enduring the deepest cut of all, the loss of what he thought of as 'his' library, but which had, in all fairness, also been such an important part of their honeymoon years for Ivy.

On 8 May 1924, Ransome and Evgenia were married in the British Consulate in Reval. 'I have got one of the staunchest and most capable wives that any man could wish for,' he wrote to Edith soon afterwards. 'Remember that I say that not in the midst of any hectic idiocy of falling in love but after six years of close partnership and friendship.' They went straight from the Consulate to the shipyard, carrying the enormous tin barrel of paint that Arthur had brought with him to the wedding to save time. After two nights at home, he set off to watch over *Racundra*'s relaunch; Evgenia joined him a day later. They left Reval on 15 May, and arrived at Riga seven days later; this time, their crew was an English friend, Lieutenant Steele. Then they spent a month in Moscow, the last time that Evgenia would see her family in Ransome's lifetime.

On 1 August, they set sail on a honeymoon cruise to explore the sheltered waters of tributaries of the Dvina River, a 'fascinating,

Evgenia and Arthur brewing up in the Baltic

mysterious, romantic and claustrophobic maze of shallow narrow channels'. Arthur fished and watched birds contentedly, but Evgenia was restive, and the weather turbulent. On 4 September, scufflings were heard in the cabin, and she discovered that the socks she had been darning had been shredded by tiny teeth. 'The cruise has ended or is on point of death,' ran Arthur's log. 'I am alone in *Racundra*, or rather not quite alone. I am alone with a mouse which has sent the whole six-foot three of the Cook, undaunted hitherto by anything but calms, in headlong flight to Riga.' Evgenia came back a little shamefacedly the next day with several mousetraps.

Two days later they tied up in the Riga yacht club. *Racundra* was taken on shore and packed away for the winter. The dream of sailing in her to England was shattered by Arthur's health, Evgenia's lack of enthusiasm and the difficulty of finding a crew. They set off for England by train and steamship. In 1925, when they needed cash for their first home in England, *Racundra* was sold to Adlard Coles with the proviso that he change her name; in *Close-Hauled* (1926), he describes sailing '*Annette II*' back to England from the Baltic.

THE LAKE IN THE NORTH
(1925–36)

LOW LUDDERBURN

'He rejoices to be, at last, anchored, not temporarily, to wait for a tide, but for ever, with his anchor's flukes sunk deep in the rusty mass of ancestral institutions. He tells himself he is no longer a rolling stone, but is settled down to gather comfortable moss.'
Arthur Ransome, 'On Becoming a Freeholder', Manchester Guardian, *19 October 1929*

After their return in mid-February, Arthur and Evgenia began to look for somewhere to live. His position at the *Guardian* meant that he could at last afford to live in his heartland, and when they saw Low Ludderburn, it was love at first sight. It is an ancient farmhouse 600 feet above sea level. 'From the terrace in front of the house you can see Arnside and a strip of sea under the Knott,' Arthur wrote to his mother. 'Water from a Roman well just behind the house . . . a lot of apples, damsons, gooseberries, raspberries, currants, and the whole orchard white with snowdrops and daffodils just coming.' They bought it the same day.

The house was shrouded by enormous yew trees, and its beams were very low, but the upstairs ceilings could be raised into the attic space to give better headroom, and the decrepit lean-to converted into a fine kitchen. 'It's a stout place, with walls two foot six thick and liveable in almost at once.' The fell above the

Watercolour of Low Ludderburn, by Edith Ransome

well looked out on what Arthur considered 'the best panorama of Lake mountains, from Black Combe to Helvellyn, and the high ground above the valleys of Lune and Eden'. The great stone barn built into the hill a few yards from the cottage had an upper storey that, once refloored and given a chimney breast instead of doors to the road and large windows with wide sills, would be a splendid place for Arthur to write.

On 27 May they moved in. Arthur wrote an exultant letter to Edith: 'We cooked our first meal, a haddock, in the fish-kettle on the Perfection Stove, a great success. There is a lovely log fire roaring up the chimney, using the rotten beams from the barn, which is now being altered. The lamp is burning on the table, under a sort of inverted soap-dish fixed above to prevent it from setting the low ceiling on fire. In a jam-pot are narcissi and bluebells from the garden. Our potatoes are in.'

The lamp on the table is a reminder that rural domestic arrangements in the late 1920s were spartan. A huge rainwater tank beside the barn could usually be counted on for water, saving the uphill traipse to the well. There was an outside earth closet. Food was kept cool in an outdoor cupboard with thick stone walls and a wire-mesh door. There was neither electricity nor telephone.

Arthur and Evgenia may well have hoped to have children, but although she was only thirty-one when they arrived at Low Ludderburn, this was not to be. A neighbouring farmer gave them a silver-grey tabby cat that promptly had three kittens, and Evgenia delighted in sketching them and their antics. They were so pretty that they drove them all the way down to the Crystal Palace Cat Show, where they won a 'highly commended'. The mother and one kitten were given away, but Polly and Pudge stayed for good.

BELOW
LEFT 'The finest workroom I ever had': watercolour of the barn at Low Ludderburn by Edith Ransome
RIGHT The legal conveyance that transferred Low Ludderburn to the Ransomes in 1925

OPPOSITE
LEFT Evgenia's sketch of Ransome in his favourite chair
RIGHT Steps up to Ransome's workroom in the barn

A reliable car was an essential accessory to life at Low Ludderburn, preferably one that Evgenia could drive, because she was often alone there. Their first car was bought in May 1925; its make is unknown. In August 1926 they acquired a Clyno 13. Later,

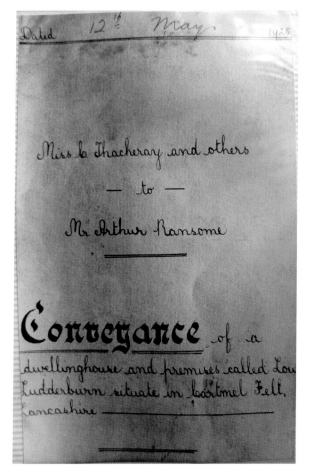

they acquired a chain-driven Trojan, which was perfect for the steep hill up to Ludderburn. It had a cloth hood and pneumatic tyres, an improvement on the early solid tyres that made Trojans such bone-shakers on rough roads. They kept the Clyno because Evgenia found the Trojan hard to drive; it was also better for long journeys.

When the barn conversion was complete, Ransome revelled in 'the finest workroom I have ever had'. He could stride around to his heart's content. 'There is a solemnity, a portentousness about sitting down to think that is itself enough to banish thought,' he wrote in his new weekly *Guardian* column 'Drawn at a Venture' for 29 July 1929. 'A man who sits down to think gets up again in a hurry, if he is not ready to mistake mooning for thinking. Quick as he may be, he gets up both physically and mentally duller than he sat down. Two turns from the window and back again will serve his purpose better than sitting for an hour. "My thoughts are prone to sleep if I sit long," wrote Montaigne. He

meant, of course, sitting in a chair. On horseback he could think well enough. A bed, a bath, our boots, a walking-stick, a horse, a bicycle, a sailing boat, our ordinary work – all these are better aids to thought than a chair.'

In summer, Ransome arranged his table just to one side of the western window, so that he could see Whitbarrow. In winter, the table was moved closer to the centre of the room and a little backwards, so that his back would be warmed by the stove, and he could see Cartmel Fell. Although his mother sent him his father's desk in 1930, he preferred to work at a large table covered with a green baize cloth. To his left was a very large waste-paper basket. Close by was a choice of pipes, a jar of tobacco and matches, a jar of penholders and a box of nibs (he disliked fountain pens), an antique Russian ink-well, a large blotter with his initials stamped on one leather corner, seal and sealing wax, his diary and current notebooks. Also on the table was a motley collection of

THE WORLD OF ARTHUR RANSOME

THE Trojan CAR

The CAR that
sees you "through"

mementoes of friends, relations and adventures in the past. A pair of travelling candlesticks and a wooden ashtray in the shape of a duck with a deep hole in its back both came from Russia, as did the Negretti and Zamba compass he had first used on *Slug*. It and his pencils, with Turk's-head knots around them to prevent them rolling away, were a promise of more cruising to come.

Beside the large table was a small folding one, to which he could move either his typewriter or his reading and writing slope, depending on what he was doing. The font wheel of his typewriter could be changed for a Cyrillic one. The house's present owner, Helen Caldwell, found one in the rubbish heap, along with innumerable tins of MacLean's Stomach Powders. Gastric problems still dogged him.

Arthur's poor health meant that there were frequent emergencies, to say nothing of running out of bread or milk, but they developed a way of signalling to Colonel and Mrs Kelsall,

OPPOSITE Bowness-on-Windermere, from Wansfell

ABOVE
LEFT The chain-driven Trojan was well suited to the steep hill up to Low Ludderburn
RIGHT Evgenia in her much-loved garden at Low Ludderburn

who lived down in the valley at Barkbooth and became invaluable friends. A white-painted wooden square and triangle could be hoisted at a variety of angles up the side of the Kelsalls' barn, answered by a black square and triangle on the white south-facing wall of Low Ludderburn. With binoculars or telescope, they could be read from either 'signal station'. A square on its own meant 'I need help urgently'. The Kelsalls were also keen fishermen, and the most frequent use for the signals was to arrange angling expeditions. By 1933, a diamond and a cross had been added, and the code was of breathtaking complexity.

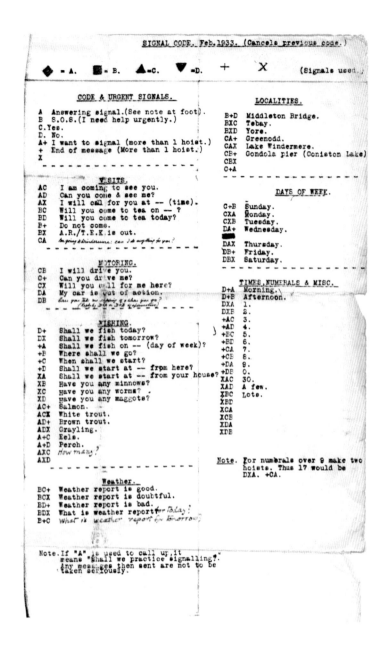

Colonel Kelsall's improved signalling code between Barkbooth and Low Ludderburn

In December 1926, Ted Scott, son of the *Guardian*'s editor C. P. Scott and fast becoming a close friend, asked Ransome to go to China. Britain was interested in knowing about Russian influence on the civil war that was under way in China between the nationalist Kuomintang and the feudal and piratical warlords. To oblige him, Ransome agreed, and spent three months there, meeting mandarins and missionaries, bankers and Bolsheviks, smacking his lips with affected appreciation over a surfeit of unappealing titbits that it would have been boorish to refuse from his hosts' chopsticks, and gathering material that would be put to good use when he wrote *Missee Lee* fifteen years later. But the trip was the last straw. In a letter to Evgenia, he wrote that he hoped that he would not be sent on any more of 'these horrible adventures . . . I am too old for them. I am all for slippers and a pipe, a glass of hot rum and the quiet life. Also I hate most horribly being away from my sterling old woman. It seems such a waste. And I hate being out of England.' He travelled home on the Siberian Express in time to enjoy the bluebells that carpeted the woods around Low Ludderburn.

Edith Ransome and the rest of the family constantly sent comforts. A letter from Arthur two days after the Christmas of 1927 thanked her effusively for a chair that was

the very ideal of all chairs. It does not repel by its self-importance. It is plain, sober as a Quaker, which gives confidence. And when you are in it, what luxury. It fits me perfectly. I can lounge in it with my feet aloft like a University student. I can sit in it with straight back, in the most comfortable of all positions for reading. It rests one instantaneously, like sleep, when tired. It simply is the chair that in all of my life I have neither had nor deserved. I can only hope that within it, I shall produce something worthy of such an origin.

THE WORLD OF ARTHUR RANSOME

INSPIRATION

'What fun it would be if I could write them a book about the Swallow and the lake and the island that was their playground, as it had been ours and that of our parents before us.'

Arthur Ransome, 'Letter to the Editor', Junior Bookshelf, *July 1937*

Living in the Lake Country meant that Arthur could resume his old friendship with the Collingwoods. WG and Dorrie were still very fond of him, but were now in their seventies, and not in good health. WG had a weak heart, and Dorrie had been an invalid for several years. But there was a new generation of Collingwoods. Early in September 1925, Arthur and Evgenia went to Ursula's marriage to Reggie Luard-Selby (later Vicar of Ambleside and Troutbeck), in Coniston Church. A fortnight later, they saw Barbara married to Oscar Gnosspelius, a half-Swedish engineer, in Hawkshead Church. Barbara and Oscar's only daughter, Janet,

was born on 18 July 1926. Dora had married Ernest Altounyan in 1915. The extrovert son of an Armenian doctor and an Irish nurse, he had been a Rugby friend of Geoffrey Ransome as well as of Robin Collingwood. Their eldest child, Taqui, was born in 1917. Since 1919, they had been living in Aleppo, where their fifth and youngest child, Brigit, was born in 1926.

On 21 April 1928 the Altounyans returned for a long visit to

LEFT Self-portrait, by Dora Altounyan
RIGHT Ernest Altounyan, by Dora Altounyan

Left to right: Susan, Taqui, Titty and Roger Altounyan in Aleppo, c.1926

At the weekend, Dora went to stay with Barbara and Oscar at Kentmere, ending with a visit to Low Ludderburn. Ernest and the children drove over to pick her up on 1 May, and it may have been then that he told Arthur about two lug-sailed dinghies he had located on Walney Island, off Barrow-in-Furness. They were both 14-footers, one with a small keel and iron pigs for ballast, the other slimmer in the beam and with a centreboard. Ransome paid half the cost, and the plan was for the roomier keel boat, which would be better suited later to two substantial anglers, to be his after the Altounyans returned to Aleppo. It was natural to call her *Swallow*; she was thus to be the third and best loved of a long line. The centreboard dinghy was called *Mavis*, a Collingwood family name shared by Ursula and Titty. Sailing lessons had to be postponed, however, as Ernest and Dora spent the next ten days in London. A few days after their return, Dorrie's health worsened. The family gathered. She died on 24 May, comforted by their presence.

Robin Collingwood lingered at Lanehead for a week, and he and Ernest had some fine sailing, taking six-year-old Roger with them for a race around Peel Island. On 1 June, the day he left, Dora and Ernest sailed to Peel Island; there is no mention of the children. The next day, Dora went to Kentmere to arrange for Barbara and Oscar to move to Lanehead in mid-July, as she and Ernest were planning a round of visits and a trip to Paris. When she came home, she records that she 'found Arthur at the boathouse', presumably watching Ernest and the children afloat. This is the only mention in Dora's diary of Arthur at Bank Ground Farm in 1928. The next morning Ernest sailed the children down to Peel Island, and Dora walked down the east side of the lake via Brantwood and joined them there for tea. They rowed home in a dead calm.

This was her last record of activities on the water. Ernest had planned a round of visits to European hospitals, and left for London the next day. He returned on 23 June, and he and Dora made a tour of the borders, ending at Stranraer, where Ernest boarded the Belfast ferry. On 9 July, the 'Gnossies' arrived, and

Coniston because Dorrie was extremely ill. Instead of introducing their turbulent presence at Lanehead, they stayed at Bank Ground Farm, five minutes' walk away through the garden gate and across a small field, and even closer to the lake. 'Ernest spent nearly all day on the lake with the children,' Dora recorded the next day. He was keen for the four older children to learn to sail. Taqui was eleven, Susan was nine, Mavis (always known as Titty) was eight and Roger, their only son, was rising seven. But the old *Swallow* was no more, *Toob* was too small and *Beetle* too heavy.

LEFT The Altounyan children and *Beetle* in the harbour of
Peel Island, c.1924
ABOVE Silk flag made by Evgenia for the new *Swallow*

two days later Ernest returned to Coniston. On 13 July, Dora took him to Manchester and then went on to London for a weekend with Robin. She returned to Coniston for the weekend of 27 July, and then left for London and Paris, where she met up with Ernest, who had been in Brittany. They took a sleeper train to Alsace and Basle, and Ernest visited hospitals. Then word came of a crisis in Aleppo, and Ernest left for Syria. Dora headed home, reaching Coniston on 23 August. Her diary is blank from then until mid-November, when she got a letter from Ernest. He eventually arrived home on 20 December.

In a talk given in 1994, Taqui recalled Barbara taking the children sailing and exploring the lake's coves and islands while Dora and Ernest were away, as she had on previous occasions. On their own, the children were not allowed to do more than potter about with oars near the shore; no sails were allowed. She remembered the Ransomes fishing, 'a benevolent presence', nearby. It is likely that Arthur came over more often after Ernest, to whom he always had an antipathy, had left, though WG's diary only records a handful of visits. Nevertheless, the mood of the *Swallows and Amazons* books, in which parents are absent and children have to act in their own right, was set.

What with settling into Low Ludderburn, researching and writing fishing articles, and travelling abroad for the *Guardian*, nothing had come of Ransome's dream of writing fiction but two short yachting yarns in the style of *Riddle of the Sands*, and a Christmas play about Aladdin for Ted Scott's daughter Peggy's school. 'Working for a daily newspaper [makes] book-writing proper impossible,' he moaned in a letter. But that summer watching children revel in being afloat on his favourite lake made all the difference. After Christmas was over, the Altounyans packed for Aleppo, staying just long enough to visit 'Unkartha' on his birthday on 16 January with the gift of a splendid pair of red Syrian slippers. In a romanticized 'Letter to The Editor' written in 1937 for *Junior Bookshelf*, Ransome says that he decided to compensate them for losing *Swallow* and thank them for the slippers by 'writing them a book all about the little *Swallow* they were leaving behind'.

SWALLOWS AND AMAZONS (1930)

'I will make, if possible, a book that a child shall understand, yet a man will feel some temptation to peruse should he chance to take it up' (Walter Scott's Diary, 10 June 1827) . . . I have always thought this a perfect description of the books I should like to have written.'

Arthur Ransome

The summer with the Altounyans summoned up visions of writing a children's book about the lake that would also celebrate his own childhood holidays there. But frequent spells of poor health and a winter so harsh that there was skating on Windermere made it hard to settle down to writing. The rainwater tank froze, as did the Roman well above the house, so water had to be carried up from a lower well. Matters came to a head on 20 February 1929, when C. P. Scott summoned Ransome to Manchester and asked him if he would become Berlin correspondent from April. The salary was enormous, £1,000 a year. But it would have meant diving back into the political world for at least two years, and the end of his dream of going back to fiction. Evgenia, loath to leave Low Ludderburn, where the garden was a sea of snowdrops and daffodils, and would soon sport Canterbury bells, foxgloves and roses galore, bravely supported his decision to turn down the offer. Developing a new source of writing income now had a new urgency.

In the third week of March, *Swallow* was put back on Windermere, 'an inland sea for a boat her size', Ransome wrote to Ted Scott, in the hope of luring him up for a sail. On the 23rd, he and Evgenia sailed down the lake to Storrs Hall pier, where they had tea, arriving back at Bowness at dusk in a failing wind. Next day, his diary entry was 'Began S&A'. The Walker children, three of whom were named after the Altounyans, are longing to sail, but their father is on his way to Hong Kong; by the end of the book they have found a substitute adult mentor in an author living on a houseboat halfway down the lake. Fat, bald-headed, fiery-tempered and only recently retired from travelling the world, he is unmistakably Ransome, his dream of being a live-aboard fulfilled.

In what may have been a conciliatory gesture to Ivy and Tabitha, Arthur made the Swallows' surname Walker, Ivy's maiden name. Who were the Amazons? Taqui, who had for artistic reasons to be replaced as the oldest Walker by John, had no doubt about who she was. 'Anyway, I enjoyed giving orders and being thoroughly

Captain Nancyish,' she wrote to Arthur in 1931. Nancy's name and her ingenuity were borrowed from the Anansi tales, which Arthur always acted out as if told by a Jamaican nurse to a 'Miss Nancy'. Peggy's name was perhaps a compliment to Ted Scott's daughter; Commander 'Ted' Walker one to Ted himself. The pin-sharp detail of the cleverly contrasting characters of the Walkers and the Blacketts was, however, all Ransome's own work, the fruit of that long apprenticeship in literature which had taught him to analyse how writers get their effects and do likewise.

Although the book is dominated by practical details of sailing and camping, laced with the language of Richard Jeffries' *Bevis*

OPPOSITE Ransome sailing in *Swallow* in Bowness Bay, Windermere

BELOW Ransome wrote five books in his upstairs workroom in the barn

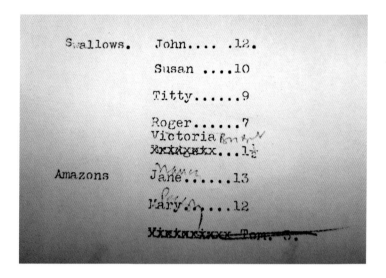

and Stevenson's *Treasure Island*, it has a classic form: a plot (the Walkers are wrongly accused of setting off a firework on the roof of the houseboat, and then, worse, of stealing from it) and a sub-plot (war with the Amazons) which merge in a climax. Like all good storytellers, Ransome denied that he could control his characters. 'They kept doing things that had not been allowed for in the Contents . . . It was as if Able Seaman Titty and Mate Susan and Captain John and Roger the Ship's Boy were pulling my fingers this way and that. It was their affair, not mine.'

Early in April, Ransome went to London for a momentous meeting with Jonathan Cape, who had published a Travellers Library edition of *Racundra's First Cruise* in 1927. Cape had said at a party the year before that he wanted to publish a collection of Ransome's fishing essays, and Ransome brought him the manuscript of what would appear in July as *Rod and Line*. He also showed him the first forty-five pages of *Swallows and Amazons*. Cape liked it, and offered him an advance of £100. He went back to Ludderburn, and alternated writing and sailing in *Swallow*,

thinking of the sailing I had had with the Walkers and remembering the lake years and years ago before they

were born, when I used to play about on it with their mother and father who were then not much bigger than the Walkers are now. I sailed and I fished and I landed on islands and made my tea and sailed again and I thought of a camp of years ago on the best of islands.

By July he had completed a rough draft, but progress slowed when Ted Scott took over editorship of the *Manchester Guardian* from his father and asked Ransome to write the paper's well-paid 1,800-word Saturday essay. The first of his witty and personal 'Drawn at a Venture' columns appeared on 13 July. Life at home was a recurrent theme. 'Dust' features Evgenia's whirlwind cleansings of his workroom, 'Inanimate Things' describes the books on his shelves as the lining of his memory, 'On Gardening' reveals that he was barely trusted to behead pansies. The book faltered even more as Arthur's health worsened. Glands swelled under his armpits, and pain from his stomach ulcer increased in intensity.

Both health and progress on the book improved dramatically when Ransome agreed to go by ship to Cairo to report on the Egyptian election. The voyage gave him plenty of sea air and long uninterrupted periods for continuing work on his story. In April, he delivered *Swallows and Amazons*. It was published on 21 July 1930. There was a glorious endpaper map by Stephen Spurrier, which was used as a cover, but Ransome rightly rejected his whimsical illustrations.

ABOVE Ransome's tentative naming of his child characters

OPPOSITE, CLOCKWISE FROM TOP LEFT:
'The ASS has forgotten the mast': Ransome's criticism of Stephen Spurrier's sketch of the houseboat
Susan by the campfire, drawn by Clifford Webb for the first illustrated edition of *Swallows and Amazons* (1931)
Arthur Ransome's 1938 illustration of the same scene
Unused dedication drawn by Spurrier for *Swallows and Amazons*; the 'four' became 'six' in the published book

What on earth is Captain Flint doing.

Page (84)

Swallows & Amazons. (The ASS has forgotten the Mast. A.R.)

THE MATE AT WORK

U

Facing p. 256

TO
the four for whom it
waf   written
in exchange
for
a

pair of flippers.

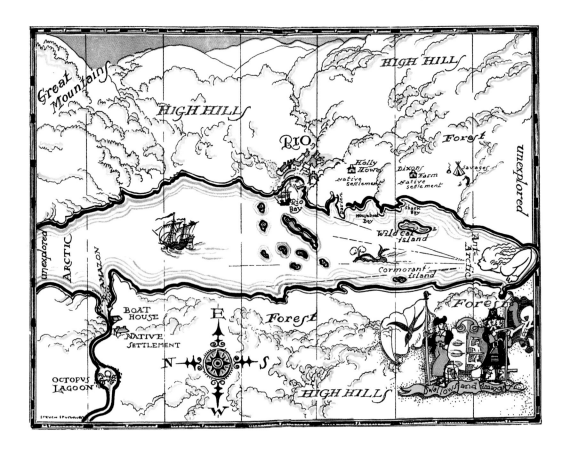

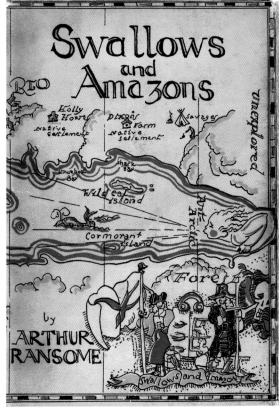

Swallows and Amazons by ARTHUR RANSOME

An early copy was sent to Aleppo. The Altounyans loved it, Ernest proudly claiming ownership of the 'damn fine sporting kids'. Edith Ransome wrote to her daughter Joyce that his letter had depressed Arthur a good deal – as it well might, ignoring as it did the fact that the book was quite as much, if not more, inspired by Ransome's long-ago holidays at Nibthwaite and Lanehead. Wild Cat Island was Peel Island, a place that Ransome had loved since he was a small boy, and as a young man he had delighted in camping alone there. Octopus Lagoon was Allan Tarn, a circular pool close to the mouth of the River Crake near Nibthwaite, where his father had often fished. There was Cyril as well as Arthur in Captain Flint – in his autobiography Arthur describes how his father refused to believe him more than once. He often felt he had been a disappointment to him, and made John the model son

ABOVE Stephen Spurrier's map of the 'Lake in the North', an amalgam of Coniston and Windermere, was used for the cover (right) as well as the endpapers (left) of the first edition of *Swallows and Amazons* (1930)

OPPOSITE
ABOVE Barbara Collingwood with the Altounyan children and their Armenian nurse sailing in *Beetle* at Coniston, c.1924
BELOW Roger, aged seven, in *Swallow*, close to the shore at Bank Ground Farm

he wished he had been. The parrot with green feathers belonged to his sister Joyce, who was just as much a romancer as Titty, and Roger's sense of fun and love of engines (themes developed in later books) were characteristics of his brother Geoffrey, killed untimely in 1918.

SWALLOWDALE (1931)

"'It's just the place for Peter Duck," said the able-seaman.
"It's the most secret valley that ever there was in the world.'"

Arthur Ransome, Swallowdale

Enthusiasm for *Swallows and Amazons* from both critics and readers was general. Visiting a London bookshop, Queen Mary bought a copy for the young princesses. 'She paid cash for it – I asked,' Ransome exulted, from his sickbed. He was spending two months in London convalescing from another bout of trouble with his duodenal ulcer. On the advice of a doctor, he had been slimming, and weighed only ten and a half stone. A new doctor issued the welcome edict that he should fatten himself up, which led to a steady improvement in his health. He also forbade the use of aluminium cooking pans, a prohibition that Evgenia zealously extended to every house they visited for a meal.

When the American publisher Lippincott and the Junior Literary Guild, an American children's book club, took the book on for a £600 advance, money worries were eased, although the economic depression meant less work from the *Manchester*

Guardian. The Ransomes had to dip into their savings, and were grateful for some financial help from Edith; they even considered selling Low Ludderburn, but fell in love with it again when they got home. 'Just as we arrived, there was a bit of sunshine and it looked so lovely that we both felt that we could never really leave it,' Arthur wrote to his mother in January. 'Genia soon had three heaters and two fires going in the house (which was surprisingly dry), and we got to bed in proper time in a cottage that was already in complete going order.'

More good news came in the shape of Cape's request for a sequel. At the age of forty-seven, Ransome was at last on course to literary success. He set to work on it once he was back in his beloved workroom. 'My notion now is to go on and on and build up a regular row of these books, if only I can make enough to live on out of them, which I think I shall,' he wrote to Ernestine Evans of Lippincott. At first he thought he would follow up by taking his plucky young crews on the *Treasure Island*-style adventure that he had begun to develop before he dreamt up *Swallows and Amazons*. It starred a thinly disguised Carl Sehmel, the omniscient mate of *Racundra*, as a wise old seaman called Peter Duck, and opened with the children and Captain Flint on a winter holiday on a wherry in the Norfolk Broads; as it is too frozen to sail, they spin a yarn of an imaginary voyage from Lowestoft in a little green schooner called *Wild Cat*: the island afloat. Cape thought otherwise: what children want in a sequel, he said, is more of the same. So the new story, which Ransome began in January 1931, opens a year after the first. Just as Ransome did when he returned

Ransome's cartoon of his fattened-up self – on doctor's orders

View of the Old Man of Coniston
and a Beckfoot-style boathouse

View of the Old Man of Coniston
and a Beckfoot-style boathouse

to Coniston, 'Titty dipped her hands in the cool water of the harbour just to show herself that she was really there.' Roger finds it more difficult to fit into the bow of *Swallow*; plans are afoot for a combined camp of the allies on Wild Cat Island. Never one to repeat himself, Ransome began to think about new developments. Desmond Kelsall recalled him asking what should happen next. 'I said that John should become over-confident in handling *Swallow* and should run her on the rocks. Arthur Ransome gave a great guffaw of laughter and said, "That's exactly what I've been thinking myself."' The Kelsall boys also helped him make the blotchy Ship's Papers, using their parrot's sooted claw.

Wrecking *Swallow* provided scope for practical advice on what to do when your dinghy is sinking, and how to repair boats. It celebrated the traditions of the Lake counties, with accounts of wrestling, sheepdog trials and hound trails ('"Won't they tear

the tents to pieces?" said Susan'). The best of the hounds is called Melody, a nod to his old friend Lascelles Abercrombie, with whom he used to quaff ale and smoke pipes at the Hark to Melody Inn, at Haverthwaite. Roger and Titty creep along the stream under a road bridge just as Arthur used to do at Nibthwaite, John and Susan are taught to fly fish by Captain Flint as he was by his father. The twelve leisurely pages of the chapter called 'Life in Swallowdale' owed much to his memories of camping near Low Yewdale.

Despite being impeded by their much-feared great-aunt, the Amazons get away to join them to climb the 2,634-foot high Old Man of Coniston, up which Ransome had been carried by Cyril Ransome as a baby. It is renamed Kanchenjunga, after the Nepalese summit ten times its height and then the goal of numerous expeditions, though still unconquered. The friendly charcoal-

Beacon Tarn, above Water Yeat, may have been the inspiration for *Swallowdale*'s Trout Tarn

burners from *Swallows and Amazons* reappear, saving the day once again when Roger twists his ankle high up on the fell by looking after him and getting Titty a lift home on the woodmen's tree-wagon. The farmers and their families play a much larger part, not just as natives helping explorers but as rounded characters with lives of their own. The Swainsons of Nibthwaite are shifted across the lake, and the children savour their lives to the full: 'The others came from the farm and told of how they had been singing choruses with old Mr Swainson, and sewing a patch into Mrs Swainson's new patchwork quilt, and seeing pigs and calves and a foal, and the biggest tabby cat that ever was seen in the world.'

Best of all there is a camp in a secret valley. Just as Wild Cat Island was a composite of the best features of several lake islands, so

Ransome gave Swallowdale, which he drew on a notebook map as nestling below Beacon Tarn to the west of Coniston Water, a stream from here and a couple of waterfalls from there until it became the best little valley in the world. It had a 'Knickerbockerbreaker' on which Roger tears his trousers just as Arthur did at Nibthwaite, and a cave for Peter Duck, the hero of the book he intended to write next.

Swallowdale was published late in October 1931, with pictures by Clifford Webb, whose illustrated edition of *Swallows and*

SWALLOWDALE

LEFT Pike Rock? A hazard off Peel Island
RIGHT Helene Carter's illustration for the American
edition of *Swallowdale* (1932)

Amazons had come out a month before. He had come up to the Lakes to be shown the locations. 'The dullest decadent coxcomb ever in this place . . . But he can draw well' runs Ransome's diary note. Good as Webb's drawings were, Ransome was dissatisfied with them, preferring the high romance of the ones that Helene Carter was doing for the American editions. Ransome was dubious about the book, but Wren Howard, Jonathan Cape's partner, wrote to say that he liked it even better than the first, as did Taqui and Titty Altounyan. W. G. Collingwood, now very frail, said he thought it just as good. Reviewing it for the *Spectator*, Naomi Mitchison wrote: 'They are real, modern, children, and those who feel gloomy for the future of England should consider that it is boys and girls like the Swallows and the Amazons who are the potential new citizens – and there is little to fear!' The Junior Guild made it its book of the year. Such praise made up for Tabitha's hurtful declaration in a letter of February 1931 that she had found *Swallows and Amazons* 'churned out and tried after', and had given up on it. Tabitha was no longer a child, but a twenty-year-old young woman, and relations with her father had steadily deteriorated because of Ivy's monitoring of her letters to her father, and veto on visits to the Lakes.

PETER DUCK (1932)

If sailor tales to sailor tunes,
Storm and adventure, heat and cold,
If schooners, islands and maroons
And Buccaneers and buried Gold,
And all the old romance, retold
Exactly in the ancient way,
Can please, as me they pleased of old,
The wiser youngsters of today:
— So be it and fall on!

Robert Louis Stevenson, Treasure Island

The success of *Swallowdale* decided Ransome to have the courage of his convictions and turn back to 'Their Own Story', the piratical romp in 'the Caribbees' that he had wanted to write after *Swallows and Amazons*. He had flagged up the idea of a story invented over the previous winter in *Swallowdale* when Titty decides that the cave she and Roger find in Swallowdale should belong to its hero, Peter Duck.

At first, it went slowly; he was still writing his weekly 'Drawn at a Venture' essay for the *Manchester Guardian*. A guinea cut in his rate decided him to end what had become a tedious chore. His guts corkscrewed ever more painfully, and when the Altounyans urged him and Evgenia to join them in Aleppo so that Ernest could work a miracle cure and the children could show him 'what we are *really* like', they decided to go. Arthur remembered how much progress on *Swallows and Amazons* he had made on his voyage to Cairo. Evgenia wanted to eat oranges off trees.

The sea air and the absence of worries worked their usual magic. Ransome made notes on the voyage down the Channel, and sketched a little green two-masted schooner in Alexandria. At Ernest's request, they brought with them a huge crate holding a

10-foot sailing dinghy, which the Altounyans named *Peter Duck* in honour of the new book. Ransome was installed in Dora's tower room in early February 1932, and in the next six weeks, with *Treasure Island* and the *Channel Pilot* by his side, he wrote over three hundred pages. He worked until the midday dinner gong went, and then read what he had written to the children in the afternoon. As the book was supposed to be a story told by Captain Flint's young crew, he decided that the illustrations would be by them too; some at least were. 'Titty AB is working hard and helping me to produce pictures for the new book,' he wrote to Ted Scott. 'She is most comically like her imaginary self. Ditto Roger. The others have rather shot up with the years.' Indeed they had; Taqui was now sixteen. She remembers Ransome playing tennis with them, and telling them Anansi stories to tunes on his penny whistle.

Progress slowed in April. The dream holiday developed into a nightmare. Ernest's cures failed, and Arthur's health worsened; Evgenia blamed the Altounyans' aluminium pans. The increasing heat was oppressive, bringing fears of all manner of diseases, and Evgenia and Ernest locked horns over the subject of the children's

education, with Ernest bristling at the idea that they were growing
up as young savages and ought to go to English schools. Dora and
Arthur sat by miserably. 'I am beginning to hanker dreadfully after
Low Ludderburn,' Arthur wrote to his mother. 'The remaining
100 pages need a lot of spirit and jump and at the minute I haven't
got any.' Then Dora went down with malaria. The Ransomes fled,
taking a ship to Cyprus, where they managed to get berths aboard
the same merchantman in which they had arrived, and enjoyed its
leisurely progress.

In Rotterdam they received appalling news: Ted Scott had
drowned when his dinghy, *Pimpernel*, capsized on Windermere.
He had bought it on Ransome's recommendation that it was
unsinkable, and it was; but whereas his son Dick clung to the hull,
Ted tried to swim to shore in the icy April water, and had a heart
attack. Ransome was shattered, and racked with guilt, though he
deserved none. He could not bear to go sailing on the lake for
three months. He had lost his best friend. 'It was as if our world
had come suddenly to an end.'

When they returned early in May, Ransome went to Lowestoft,
to get colour for the opening chapter of the book, and Evgenia went

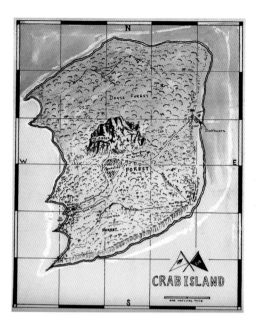

Ransome's watercolour sketch of Crab Island was
simplified for *Peter Duck* (1932)

north to Low Ludderburn to find the front door open, the larder
raided and mice everywhere. Fortunately, nothing of value had
been taken, and the thief was caught when he tried to put Chinese
coins in a slot machine. Ransome did not get back to work for
three weeks, but then revision went quickly. He abandoned the
frame of a story being told, tightened up the book's baggy middle,
and posted the typescript to the printers on 3 August.

Next, he set to work on the illustrations, using 'hollywoods' –
photographs of friends' children posing – as guides. The pencil
sketches for these in his notebooks, which have been carefully
analysed by Roger Wardale in *Ransome the Artist*, show that he had
a shrewd eye for design, and a sensitive pencil. The characterful
simplicity of the final drawings proved so successful that from
then on he illustrated all the books. By now financially canny, he
told Cape that he 'expected to be paid at professional rates', and

was. He consistently avoided showing faces, something that saved
a great deal of trouble, and which he justified playfully on the
grounds that 'There are savage tribes who think it is unlucky to
have their portraits made. My characters belong to those savage
tribes, and so it is only fair that I should guard them from falling
under the evil eye of the author. Nancy, my chief collaborator,
heartily agrees with me.' While waiting for the proofs of the
finished book, Arthur enjoyed fishing and sailing, competing
with Evgenia in the last of the 'Allcomers' races on Windermere
in conditions so wet and blustery that *Swallow*'s mast cracked and
they were thoroughly soaked.

Peter Duck owes much to *Treasure Island*, but even more to
E. F. Knight's *The Cruise of the Falcon*, in which Knight and his
friends sail to South America and back, coming across a remote
surf-lashed volcanic island with a coral reef around it, and his
Cruise of the Alerte, in which he sails to Trinidad in search of
treasure buried by pirates, with a map passed on by an opium
trader. Masefield's shanties lace *Peter Duck* as they did *Swallows
and Amazons*, and the quote at the head of Chapter 1 was from
his cousin Laurence Binyon's wonderful poem 'John Winter': 'He
turns his head, but in his ear/The steady trade-winds run,/And in
his eye the endless waves/Ride on into the sun.'

Peter Duck was published on 12 October, and Hugh Walpole
wrote a generous review for the *Observer* that mended the
friendship from which Ransome had shied away in Russia. The
book was reprinted almost immediately, which shows how right
Ransome had been as to the perennial appeal of pirates and
Caribbean treasure. 'The turn of the tide had come just in time to
save us and to justify Evgenia's courage in risking financial disaster.
Presently the sales of the first two books began to catch up those
of *Peter Duck* and I knew I could afford to write another.' Treasure
had indeed been found. It was an added bonus that his ulcers
had subsided; if he avoided the stress of newspaper deadlines, his
doctor thought they would remain quiescent.

ABOVE AND RIGHT
Ransome's photograph of Colonel
Kelsall and children for (right) a
drawing for *Peter Duck*
FAR RIGHT Ransome's drawing
of the galley of the invented
schooner *Wild Cat*

WINTER HOLIDAY (1934)

'Frozen Windermere is indeed a marvel! The ice, except in the bays, is always harder and smoother than usual, and keen steels add to the pleasure of travel. At such time one feels the expanse of lake more than when boating . . . at night the skater seems to move in a hushed circle . . . the moonlight and loneliness and silence act as a spell.'

William Palmer, The English Lakes, *1908*

Ransome envisaged *Peter Duck* as the last book about the Swallows and the Amazons, partly on the advice of Helen Ferris, of the American Junior Literary Guild. Congratulating him on scoring an unprecedented hat-trick when it was chosen as the JLG's book of the year, she wrote, 'Why don't you do something entirely different with a new set of youngsters? . . . I think it would be a very good idea, both from the business point of view and from the sheer fun you would have tackling new material.' But soon after this, some young American fans sent him a letter and a bunch of

photographs illustrating their adventures on a frozen lake in New England, romantically captioned with the names of legendary places. The letter (which has not survived) was an important catalyst, and *Winter Holiday* is dedicated to 'The Clan McEoch'. Arthur had after all known his 'Lake in the North' deep frozen not once but twice. The first time was as a schoolboy in 1894/5. He had impressed his friends with his competence at skating, seen a coach and four gallop across the lake, watched an ox being roasted on the ice and admired Herbert Crossley's ice yachts

LEFT Sketch of tarn and skaters by Edith Ransome, adapted by Ransome for *Winter Holiday* (1933)

OPPOSITE Evgenia walking round an ice-bound yacht in the winter of 1929

racing ('There were three or four of them rushing about the lake in '95, and racing for a silver cup,' reminisces Mrs Dixon). The second time was in 1929, when he and Evgenia skated around a frozen-in houseboat.

Another adventure on the Lake in the North meant that all thoughts of doing away with the Swallows and Amazons were dismissed. The bonus of setting a real adventure in the winter was that it prevented his fictional children from growing up too fast. He settled down to write in early January 1933, cleverly giving Nancy mumps so that quarantine meant an extension of the short winter holidays to a month of quarantine, and sketching out skating lessons, a night in the frozen houseboat and a sailing sledge, using his memories of the frozen Baltic wilderness and ice yachts skimming across the Stint See. But his outline was short both on action and plot. He decided to introduce two completely new characters, personalities in their own right who offered a useful new angle of approach to both the lake and the six young heroes and heroines of the previous three books.

Enter Dick the scientist and Dorothea the romancer, each exhibiting a different side of Ransome's own character, as well as being tributes to his lost brother Geoffrey and his very literary-minded sister Joyce. Ransome may also have had in mind

ABOVE LEFT Ice yacht designed by Crossley of Windermere
ABOVE Ransome's photograph of children hauling a 'sledge'; his Trojan car can be seen in the background
LEFT Drawing of a sailing sledge from Fridtjof Nansen's *Farthest North*

E. Nesbit's *The Wouldbegoods* (1899), in which two new characters, Daisy and Denny, nervously join the confident Bastables, but soon prove their worth; her book has a chapter called 'Being Beavers, or the Young Explorers (Arctic or Otherwise)', in which Oswald experiments with a romantic literary style closely kin to Dorothea's. In one of the most effective openings of any of his books, Ransome has the two Ds 'signalling to Mars' from their 'Observatory', a barn above Dixon's Farm, to the distant children they can see busy in boats on the lake near Holly Howe. The jaunt to High Greenland was inspired by Nansen's earlier *First Crossing of Greenland*. Ransome had met the famous Norwegian explorer and peace envoy in Riga in 1921. It was natural to follow it with a quest for the Pole, achieved by Nansen in 1893, when Arthur was nine. '"Here it is", said Dick. "*Farthest North: The Voyage and*

Exploration of the Fram *and the Fifteen-Months Sledge Expedition.* This'll tell us everything we want to know."' Their igloo made use of a stone hut as did that of the Norwegians at their Spitzbergen base camp. The Pole itself was to be sited, according to Ransome's notes for the book, in 'a bathing hut at the head of the lake'. There were two of these at the time, one rectangular, one contrived from the superstructure of an old paddle-steamer.

Winter set in while he was roughing out the story. The Altounyan girls were now at school in Windermere, and at the end of January he took them skating on Duck Tarn, above Low Ludderburn, and on Tarn Hows. 'Sunshine,' he noted in his diary. 'Snow on hills, but only on top. Titty kicking with only one leg.' In February, he told Wren Howard that the new book 'was a thick and discouraging fog'. Then disaster struck. 'Prancing along in great good cheer' down the steep and at that time icy hill from Low Ludderburn to the ford by the Winster road, he slipped and fell. He broke an ankle and almost a knee, and had to crawl home. But perhaps because he was confined to bed and chair, progress on the story improved. 'It is beginning to feel more like a story,' he wrote to his mother on 27 February. 'One at least of the two new characters you won't be able to help liking. I find her a most entertaining companion, and in fact I more than half owe my broken ankle to listening to her conversation instead of watching my feet.' The accident made the signals to the Kelsalls more useful than ever, and they found their way into *Winter Holiday*.

For all the fluency of the finished book, it was a long haul. He spent the whole of the summer struggling with it and its illustrations. The fact that they were suffering from a drought, with water running short, the garden 'mostly brown tinder' and farmers haymaking by moonlight to spare the horses the heat of the day, made writing about a great frost 'a fearful strain on faith'.

Ransome celebrated *Winter Holiday*'s delivery to Cape at the end of August with a sail in *Swallow*, flying the new silk flag that Evgenia had made for her. After the proofs had been vetted, he hired a motor cruiser on the Broads for a late September fishing holiday with his friends Charles and Margaret Renold, 'with a sailing dinghy in case there is any backsliding on my part'. While hoisting sail in Potter Heigham, Arthur was struck down with severe appendicitis. Fortunately, there was an excellent surgeon in Norwich. Arthur began his convalescence at the King's Head Hotel in Wroxham, where he could fish and watch the boating world go by from the lawn.

Winter Holiday was published on 13 November 1934. Five thousand copies were sold in the first month, and it was immediately reprinted. Cape naturally commissioned a sequel, and Arthur's old friend Herbert Hanson, secretary of the Cruising Association, suggested he went to St Mawes, in Cornwall, to convalesce and plan it. On 18 November, Arthur and Evgenia

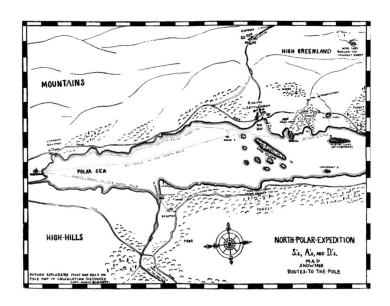

Ransome's endpaper map for *Winter Holiday*

took the steamship *Southern Coast* from London to Falmouth. They took lodgings for six weeks in St Mawes at the Watch House, a seventeenth-century house with views both up the creek towards Truro and across the harbour to the open sea. It had originally been used as a lookout for sailing ships in need of pilot gigs. It also looked over Hanson's huge sailing barge *Industry*, which was being refitted there. With his financial prospects so much more secure, Arthur began to dream of once again having a sea-going boat. Relations also improved between him and Ivy, who was now living in Falmouth. Although they did not meet, Tabitha came to visit. He still wanted his books back, but it is clear that Ivy and Tabitha treasured them. A special extension for them was built when Ivy moved to a bungalow in Bishopsteignton, looking over the Teign estuary.

PIGEON POST (1936)

"'A Pigeon a Day keeps the Natives Away.'"
Nancy Blackett, in Arthur Ransome, Pigeon Post

The Ransomes left Falmouth on a Liverpool-bound steamer in early January, and settled back into Low Ludderburn. Arthur had decided that his next book would be set in the Broads, with a brand-new cast. There will be more about *Coot Club* when we consider Ransome afloat; here we are concerned with his last year at Low Ludderburn, and the writing of *Pigeon Post*.

A letter written to Tabitha in April 1934 hinting at earlier amicable exchanges suggests that father and daughter were now on better terms, perhaps because she had moved away from home. He must have mentioned the idea of getting a bigger boat to her, as he says that he has not got one yet; then he describes a race round Belle Isle between himself in *Swallow* and his friends the Renolds in *Coch-y-Bonddhu*, the fishing dinghy, named for a trout fly, that he had persuaded them to have built. He and Evgenia had a new kitten, 'with the face of an angel and a heart packed tight with mischief', and Low Ludderburn was so covered with daffodils that even sending 'baskets and baskets (really shoeboxes and shoeboxes) away' and filling the church with them made no impact on the quilt of tossing flowers.

Soon after this, the Ransomes had three weeks on the Broads checking the details of *Coot Club*, and then lingered in London catching up with friends. Returning to remote and primitive Low Ludderburn was beginning to feel like exile, and the vision of moving out solidified. With an eye to selling, they began to smarten it up. 'The place is looking simply perfect,' Edith Ransome wrote to Joyce in August. 'Genia has got the garden and entrance so nice. The road has been well-repaired and is quite good for cars now.'

Arthur's relations with Tabitha faltered when she sent him a letter saying that she had married a 'Dock Labourer', and that they were in Paris. She had inherited her mother's taste for drama; Frederick Harold Lewis, though something of a maverick and very young, was in fact a resourceful boat builder. Arthur replied with a pompous letter of advice on how to be a good wife, all deeply felt and much of it sound, but unlikely to be well received. He ended it with an invitation for her to come and stay so that she could 'see the sort of life that is lived here, and the country that has been the background of people of your race for a very long time indeed'. She never came.

The year 1935 began inauspiciously when, after a trip to Devon to look at boats in Brixham and to discuss Tabitha over lunch with Ivy (who had mendaciously claimed that Lewis was deformed and half-witted), Arthur skidded on ice and rolled the car over near Hereford. Luckily, he suffered only a bruised knee and a cut leg. His fatherly anxiety was lessened when Ivy wrote revising her earlier judgment and saying that Lewis 'has all the decent instincts . . . he never takes advice amiss, he is never presumptuous, nor cringing – just natural'. She also generously said she would limit her financial claim on Arthur to £100 a year, rather than the third of his income originally agreed, and that she would hand it on to Tabitha. Perhaps she had inherited money from her parents. She signed this letter 'Your placid ex-wife Constance'. Relations between them remained amicable until her premature death at the age of fifty-seven in 1939.

In February, Ransome settled down in earnest to planning *Pigeon Post*, which had its initial inspiration in Barbara's husband

The New Camp

Oscar Gnosspelius' 1929 discovery of a new vein of copper under the shoulder of Brim Fell above Coniston. Copper had been mined there until the early years of the century; in his autobiography Ransome recalls seeing barges carrying copper ore down the lake when he was a boy. Legend had it that in Elizabethan times there had also been gold, and nothing less will do for the young prospectors. The Gnossies now lived at High Hollin Bank, very close to Lanehead. On 17 February, Ransome's diary records that Oscar, who would be metamorphosed into Squashy Hat, came to tea, and was 'full of help about the mining'. On 27 March, Oscar took him up the Tilberthwaite Valley. 'Saw several of the old workings and a suitable bit of country for my story,' Ransome recorded in his diary. He also met John 'Willie' Shaw, whom Oscar had set up quarrying slate once copper proved unprofitable;

he appears in the story as Slater Bob. Shaw told him about the way through to the other side, a route which involved far more descending and ascending shafts than the tunnel explored by the 'hurrying moles' in *Pigeon Post*.

Homing pigeons, the mobile phones of their day, had long been used by the quarrymen to send messages to both their families and the head office in Keswick; they also bring to mind Ransome's early passion for taming white mice. He asked Dick Kelsall to devise the wired alarm system that signals their return. He had fun with the time-hallowed trick of dowsing for water, shrewdly allowing the sensitive Titty, rather than the over-confident Nancy, to succeed in finding the spring that makes the camp high on the fell possible. Oscar explained how to use a blowpipe to melt the ore, and Janet posed for a planned sketch of Nancy puffing furiously. In the event,

Ransome's photograph of Janet, daughter of Barbara and
Oscar Gnosspelius, posing with blowpipe

Ransome used another, showing her using a pestle and mortar.

By the middle of the summer of 1935, Ransome had finished a rough draft of *The Grubbers*, as *Pigeon Post* was originally titled. But domestic life was unsettled. Low Ludderburn was on the market. Excellent book sales, and a cruise from Portsmouth in Hanson's 7-ton yacht *Ianthe*, had encouraged them to look for a new home and a cruising boat on the east coast. Evgenia was the moving spirit in leaving the Lakes for the east coast, and it was she who identified the Shotley peninsula as both inexpensive and ideally located for sailing. Pin Mill, on the south bank of the Orwell 7 miles downstream of Ipswich, was a most attractive little yachting centre.

Edith was doubtful. 'They have not found a house in Essex yet,' she wrote to Joyce on 20 July in a letter that betrayed her true feelings about her daughter-in-law. ''Genia's ideas are so lordly,

I don't know how they are going to manage (preserve me from foreigners). She is determined to have electric light and power and hot and cold water and a big house and two servants! Poor Arthur! And he loves the Lake country and was so pleased to get back to it from Essex.'

She may not have known that Ransome was now earning £1,000 a year from royalties. Nor was it unreasonable for Evgenia to hanker after a roomier home and modern conveniences. But she was right about Ransome's love of his present home. Even as Evgenia was readying Ludderburn for sale, a nostalgia-filled Arthur was telling the readers of *The Junior Book of Authors* that

I live in a cottage more than three hundred years old high up on a hillside. I can see forty miles from my cottage door. The lakes I knew best as a boy are close at hand, and, on the nearest of them, a little boat, *Swallow*, lies at her moorings and sails as well as ever she did. There is a long row of fishing rods hanging in the cottage, like the pipes of an organ, people say.

When there is news that the rivers are in good trim, I usually manage to take a rod and go down the hill to one or another of them. This very day, the moment I have put this letter into its envelope, I shall be off to fish a river that was fished by my father long before I was born, and by my grandfather before him.

On 24 July the Ransomes looked over Broke Farm, a plain red-brick house in Levington, Suffolk. It had fine views of the Orwell River and Pin Mill, as well as a glimpse of the open sea, and they arranged to rent it from December. Cape reluctantly agreed to postpone publication for a year, so the only Ransome published in 1935 was a leather-bound pocket edition of *Old Peter's Russian Tales*. Arthur also began work on his own illustrations for *Swallowdale*; he would later complete a set for *Swallows and*

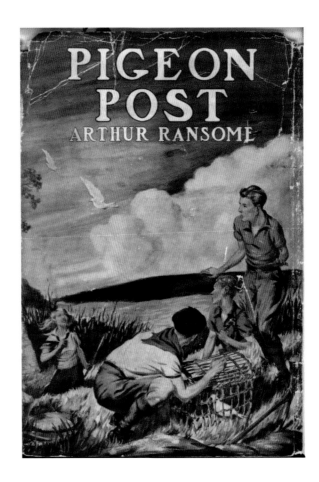

LEFT Ransome's drawing of the pigeon loft, *Pigeon Post* (1936)
RIGHT Mary E. Shepard's dust jacket for the American edition
of *Pigeon Post*

Amazons as well. The final revision of *Pigeon Post* was not begun until February 1936, 300 miles from the countryside in which it was set. Perhaps this is what encouraged Ransome to make it so rich in reference to the traditional ways of the home of his heart. 'Terribly homesick for Low Ludderburn,' he wrote in his diary for 22 April. 'I am written out and done with.'

Given all these disturbances, and nautical distractions (of which more anon), it was a triumph to send off the finished typescript to Cape on 22 August 1936, and to Lippincott a week later. *Pigeon Post* was published on 13 November, and sold every bit as well as its predecessors. It was the sixth Ransome in succession to be taken on by the Junior Literary Guild. In 1937, it received the ultimate accolade: it was the first winner of the Carnegie Medal, a new award by the Library Association for the best children's book of the year. He collected it in Scarborough from William Temple, then Archbishop of York, in front of an audience of 1,200 people, and found himself 'dithering with fright'. He enjoyed gossiping with Temple, who had been at Rugby with him, and who shared his love of detective stories, but he remained disappointed that the medal was not gold – that would, after all, have been most apt.

THE BROADS

200 MILES SAFE INLAND WATERWAYS

HOLIDAYS AFLOAT £4 PER WEEK

IT'S QUICKER BY RAIL

AT HOME AFLOAT

THE NORTHERN RIVER PIRATES

'We tacked and tacked and quanted and quanted till we came in sight of Wroxham, and in the excitement of crying "Land, land", and smacking our parched lips, we were nearly rammed by a convoy of Hullabaloos towed by a motor launch.'

George Russell's log of his 1938 cruise with the Ransomes

Despite his reputation as a sailing man, Arthur Ransome never sailed far from home, and his cruising ambitions would always centre on where a comfortable night could be spent. When he sold *Racundra* to finance the purchase of Low Ludderburn in 1925, he still had hopes of going to sea again with Evgenia in a ship of their own when money and time allowed. For the next seven years, it was impossible. There was not only the matter of money; there was also the manner in which Ransome earned it. Weekly columns, assignments abroad and drop-of-a-hat demands for leaders made it difficult to plan to 'go foreign'. Worse, there was his increasingly uncertain health. 'I did not feel I had the right to take my wife to sea, knowing that any minute I might turn into a useless passenger.' From 1931, he found the perfect substitute in 'the mild form of cruising that can be enjoyed on the Norfolk Broads'.

Poster of cruising on the Broads

There is no doubting the domestic appeal of cruising on the Broads: no turbulent seas, night watches or missed meals. The cabins of the hired yachts were spacious, comfortable and ingeniously arranged. For their first Broads holiday together, just after Easter in 1931, the Ransomes hired the two-berth *Welcome* from Herbert Woods of Potter Heigham. 'Una-rigged, with a gaff sail and the mast close to her bows, she drew so little water that she could make her way up any ditch, and in her we explored thoroughly the whole of the Broads north of Yarmouth.' It was a good time to go: best for birds, and before the holidaymakers in motor-cruisers were on the water in any numbers. Ransome persuaded Ted Scott and his son Dick to hire *Welcome*'s sister ship *Winsome*. 'We are back with copper noses that would do credit to South Sea buccaneers,' he wrote to his mother on 5 May. Despite his head being thwacked by the boom, and both the Scotts falling overboard (on separate occasions), they toured the whole of the Northern Rivers, ending with two days of 'grand sailing against a south-easterly buster with terrific rainsqualls'.

In April 1933, despite Arthur's having crocked his ankle earlier that year, he and Evgenia hired one of the new 24-foot 'Fairway' class from Jack Powles of Wroxham, revelling in its lifting cabin roof and more spacious interior. This time they had two weeks. Colonel Kelsall and his sons came with them in another Fairway, and Herbert Hanson joined them for a day. There was much signalling, not all of it understood by Evgenia. 'Jolly sick our yeoman of signals was not up to his job,' moaned Arthur, but the cook triumphed both in rowing them off the mud and in pushing the Fairway up narrow stretches with the quant. '*Welcome* did very well in the shallows, but she could not equal our quant,' crows the log. Evgenia also made celery soup, fried an eel which Arthur caught and, joy of joys, managed a chicken, then a rare treat. Just how Amazonian she could be is illustrated by a sardonic entry in the log on 17 May: 'By this time my hat, my sailing, my boom, my ears, my quanting and my steering were all wrong, so Genia took over completely.'

ABOVE Ransome playing his penny whistle and Evgenia checking her stores during a cruise on the Broads

OPPOSITE
LEFT Titty Altounyan hoists a flag
RIGHT The Northern River pirates' fleet
BELOW RIGHT Ransome hoisting a Jolly Roger

Even after Ransome had moved to Suffolk and was cruising salt water in boats of his own, he took holidays on the Broads. Autumn weeks concentrated on fishing, and were in motor-cruisers. Their gentle progress was ideal for reflecting on plot ideas, and the calm waters and roomy cabins ideal for writing. In October 1937, they hired *Royal Star* from Wroxham to fish the Thurne. The initial stages of this trip made Arthur decide that pike fishing should dominate *The Big Six*. This holiday, like his 1934 one with Charles Renold, ended prematurely when Ransome collapsed with an umbilical hernia and was rushed to Norwich hospital.

The late spring voyages were always in cabin yachts. The Kelsalls, the Renolds (with their pug William, who appears in *Coot Club*) and Molly Hamilton were among the friends who sailed with them again and again. So did a varied host of teenage children, among them many new acquaintances from Pin Mill. The years 1938 and 1939 both saw small fleets leave Wroxham, all flying Jolly Rogers, and including Taqui, Titty and Roger Altounyan. George Russell's lively log of the 1938 voyage is a treasure trove of domestic incident. 'Carried out a deep-laid plot to photograph the admiral's response to the mate's whistle from the galley . . . I rowed Mrs Ransome up to Ludham Bridge where she advised John [Young] in his shopping after he had slipped up over some veal . . . received an invitation to supper with the Ransomes which we accepted with alacrity . . . plum pudding, cold tongue, tomatoes and hot potatoes. The rum came out of its retirement.'

COOT CLUB (1934)

'They wriggled round the table and through the little folding door into the cabin that was to be their own.
On each side was a bunk spread with thick red blankets.
"May we lie down, just to try?" said Dorothea . . .
"Electric light", said Dick, turning the switch on and off. "How do they manage it in such a little boat?"'

Arthur Ransome, Coot Club

After the successful holidays in Norfolk, it was natural to plan a book set on the Broads. Ransome mused on it while he was convalescing in November 1933, first at Wroxham and then in St Mawes. 'I wish I had a good plot for my next book,' he wrote to his mother on 1 December from St Mawes. 'It is to be placed on the Broads, with all those rivers, and hiding places in the dykes and the little stretches of open water. Really a lovely setting, with herons and bitterns, and fish, very wild except just in the holiday months. But, as usual, though I have five youthful characters and one old lady, I haven't the glimmering of a plot.' At first he was planning entirely new characters: a pair of 'Propers' who are contrasted with a clutch of knowledgeable 'riversiders' dedicated to protecting birds from thoughtless holidaymakers.

His notes and letters show that he knew just what to do to make the story work. 'Concentrating the whole interest on ONE character, in the manner honoured by time and by almost all tellers of stories for boys, is easy, but it doesn't meet my views. I must have a combination of collective interest and a fair share of the game for all the individuals, girls and boys. One character ought to be concentrated local knowledge, so to speak, and he should be my

LEFT Vintage postcard of the Broads

OPPOSITE
LEFT Ransome's draft sketch of *Teasel*, showing her sail plan and cabin layout
RIGHT A Yare and Bure One Design similar to that sailed by twins Port and Starboard in *Coot Club* (1934)

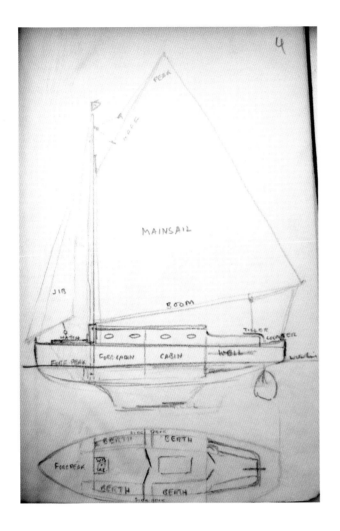

Principal Boy . . . *aet* 12 or 13 . . . living say at Horning. Then I have a pair of twins, girls, who sail with their father in a racing dinghy . . . Next property is a most spirited old lady, widow, water-colour painter, living in a ?boat or ?houseboat. She yearns to tune up her great? nieces? nephews?' The portrait of Edith was unmistakable.

But after three months of work, and a three-week cruise which provided the stormy weather that adds excitement to the *Teasel's* sail across Oulton Broad, the book was damned as 'too elaborate and too thrutched up'. On Genia's advice, he changed the Propers to Dick and Dorothea Callum. Like a Rubik cube, the plot came together. Dick and Dorothea have been sent to the Broads to stay on the *Teasel* with Mrs Barrable, their mother's one-time teacher, and are hoping to learn to sail. But she has no one to help her manage the boat. Meanwhile, six local children have formed the Coot Club to protect nesting birds. When a noisy and thoughtless gang in a huge motor-cruiser called *Margoletta* refuse to move away from a nesting coot, Tom Dudgeon, the 'principal boy', commits the unforgivable sin of untying their mooring ropes. He escapes in his little *Titmouse* (the name was borrowed from Tom Bevan's 1896 Russian thriller *Runners of Contraband*, a book from Arthur's childhood that may have gained new resonance after his and Evgenia's smuggling exploits). The 'Hullabaloos' chase after him, and he takes refuge in Mrs Barrable's *Teasel*. She asks him if he will skipper her cabin yacht and teach the Ds to sail, but he is spotted by the *Margoletta*.

The new plot changed what had been an aimless travelogue into flight from a ruthless enemy, with a splendid climax in Bredon Water when the tables are turned on the Hullabaloos: they hit a post and have to ask the Death and Glories, three intrepid sons of boat builders, also members of the Coot Club, to rescue them ('the happy ending that must almost to the end look as if it can't come off'). To add to the action, the sailing twins Port and Starboard miss the *Teasel* at Horning and hitch rides in every imaginable Broadland craft in order to catch her up. This allows Ransome to describe each boat in detail, and works 'as a fuse, delaying and therefore piling up the interest of the main theme which must for this purpose be already on its way and in the reader's mind'.

Endpaper maps which show the real geography of the Broads rather than romantic renamings, as in the Lake books, reflect the fact that elements of fantasy are all but non-existent. There are no literary tags at the chapter heads. Dorothea's vision of Tom Dudgeon as 'The Outlaw of the Broads' embarrasses him, and though the young Death and Glories still wear bright turbans and fly a Jolly Roger, the older Coots feel that piracy, 'a good plan once', has had its day. Bird protection is the thing (spotting unusual ones is a regularly recurring part of the voyage south), and by the end of the story even the young buccaneers have turned to the respectable trade of salvage.

Coot Club is Ransome's most practical story; it can be used as a handbook to the Broads. Footnotes explain unfamiliar terms like staithe, quant and rond anchor, and there is a new elegance and realism in the illustrations. Perhaps it was practice, perhaps it was the use of finer pens. In-jokes are as usual added to amuse his nearest and dearest: Mrs Barrable doodles on her letters just as he does; Dr Dudgeon attends on 'some man who has a stomach-ache and thinks appendicitis would sound better'.

THE WORLD OF ARTHUR RANSOME

As in all twelve of his children's books, Ransome shows himself to be a consummate literary technician, preparing the way for later developments with little touches that seem to be only casual asides; nor has any other novel better conveyed both the everyday atmosphere and the historic traditions of the Broads. Every kind of craft, from stately wherry and mighty Thames barge to elegant racing yachts, swift one-designs and humble punts, are brought into the story; so are eel catchers and thatchers, fishermen and boat builders, and 'oldtime marshmen who could keep their balance on a floating plank'.

The catalogue of crafts meant that Ransome could indulge his love of cabins to the full. Besides the detailed plan of *Teasel*'s interior, and his drawing of Mrs Barrable writing at its cabin table, we read of the brass hinges on the locker doors Tom acquires for *Titmouse*, Jim Woodall's cooking on *Sir Garnet*'s stove ('soft an' jewsy, that's what's good in bacon') and Mrs Whittle's red-and-white-checked tablecloth on *Welcome of Rochester* ('I like things what I call nice'). Food is as ever lovingly dwelt upon. 'Then there was the lighting of the Primus, the choosing of a tin of steak and kidney puddings, the timing of its boiling by the ship's chronometer, and then the eating of it, and of some stewed pears, several hunks of cake and some chocolate.'

Ransome remained dissatisfied with the book, especially after Evgenia damned it. In August he told Cape that the book would not be finished in time for Christmas, but Wren Howard persuaded him to change his mind with a bracing letter. 'When I last saw you, I think I said that in my view you are over particular and Mrs Ransome is hypercritical. I did not believe then and I do not believe now that the book is unpublishable, even as it stands. And I still maintain that it would be far less dangerous to let the book go to the printer now, even if it were not so highly polished as you both might wish . . . IT WILL ALL LOOK MUCH BETTER IN TYPE.' And so it did.

OPPOSITE
Always interested in domestic arrangements, Ransome showed the interiors of *Death and Glory* (left) and *Teasel*

LEFT Dust jacket by Helene Carter for the American edition of *Coot Club* (1935)

NANCY BLACKETT (1935–8)

"'I say, just look down," said Titty.
They looked down into the cabin of the little ship, at blue mattresses on bunks on either side, at a little table
with a chart tied down to it with string, at a roll of blankets in one of the bunks, at a foghorn in another, and
at a heap of dirty plates and cups and spoons in a little white sink opposite the tiny galley, where a saucepan of
water was simmering on one of the two burners of a little cooking stove.'

Arthur Ransome, We Didn't Mean To Go To Sea

Ransome's favourite photograph of *Nancy Blackett*

If the Lake Country was the country of Ransome's heart, the little ship that he loved most was the 7-ton 28-foot cutter that he renamed *Nancy Blackett*. As *Goblin*, she stars in the very best of his books, *We Didn't Mean To Go To Sea* (1936), and cruising in her gave him the setting for *Secret Water*. Built in 1931 by Hillyards of Littlehampton, she has a bowsprit and an unusual cutter rig. Her first owner gave her a suit of red sails and called her *Spindrift*; her second, a young engineer, added a suit of white sails, changed her name to the modish *Electron*, and then decided she was too small for him. Ransome called her *Nancy Blackett*, 'feeling that but for Nancy, I should never have been able to buy her'; once again one suspects that he was identifying Genia with the similarly redoubtable Amazon pirate of his imagination.

He went down to Poole to look her over on 8 September 1935, and paid the asking price of £525. Herbert Hanson found him a strong young crew in Peter Tilbury, and they set off for Pin Mill on 14 September despite a gale forecast. They romped round to Yarmouth, delighted to hear that the harbourmaster had been warned by Poole that the lifeboat might be needed to rescue them, and sat out a gale so severe that the seawall was washed away, *Nancy's* dinghy was smashed and sunk, and the lifeboat was out three times inside the harbour. Ransome acquired a storm jib in Cowes, and then went to London to sign the lease on Broke Farm and sort out insurance.

When he returned, they continued to Newhaven, and then on past Dungeness, 'carrying full sail and smoking along', taking refuge in Dover on 24 September. 'Hot baths at the Lord Warden, and ginger beer with ice in silver tankards, a most lovely drink. Steaks . . . Torrential rain . . . Got out anchor at last and steamed into Granville dock with lights playing kaleidoscopic tricks through my streaming wet spectacles.' Time was running short, and Ransome, eager to get back to help Evgenia with packing up Low Ludderburn, decided to press on. It was an exhausting voyage, and both wireless and navigation lights failed in the 'new buster' they encountered in the Thames Estuary. 'I used a red Woolworth bakelite plate with a strong torch behind it, to frighten off the Flushing Harwich steamer!!!' he wrote to Barbara and Oscar. She was, he decided, 'a wonderful little boat'.

He settled *Nancy* on a Pin Mill mooring a fortnight before Evgenia, the cats and the Kendal removal van full of Low Ludderburn's furniture, books and fisherman's clutter arrived in Levington on 18 October 1935. Broke Farm was and remains a spacious and very attractive property with splendid views, but they did not put their heart into it because they hoped to find a house on the Pin Mill side of the Orwell River. There were no loving watercolours by his mother of Broke Farm when she came to stay, though she did make a drawing, but she painted the views: Harwich, distant on the horizon, and a lonely Martello tower on the Shotley shore. 'I was waked between 3 and 4 this morning by a duet between a nightingale and a cuckoo,' she wrote to Joyce in May 1936 in a letter that held not a whisper of her earlier discontent with her daughter-in-law. 'There are some beautiful trees close to the house and the river with boats and barges seen between the trees most attractive . . . The electric light was put

ABOVE Broke Farm, Levington, was the Ransomes' first home on the east coast
BELOW View from the front garden of Broke Farm, by Edith Ransome

in yesterday. Such excitement! . . . Genia has got the house very nice and comfortable. It is all white throughout and very cheerful and airy.'

Before they left the Lakes, *Swallow* had been sold, because they had acquired the newer and faster *Coch-y-Bonddhu* from the Renolds. Sent down to Ipswich on a flatbed train truck, *Cochy* was used to row or sail over to Pin Mill. Wren Howard, Hanson and Taqui Altounyan were among the first of *Nancy*'s crews and were suitably enthusiastic. After this, she was laid up on a mud berth for the winter and Ransome took her gear to Broke Farm to work on. While Evgenia lost herself in domestic arrangements and a ferocious assault on the garden, Arthur disappeared into the usefully spacious attic to work on *Nancy Blackett*'s rig. 'I had a happy time in the attic scraping and varnishing blocks, painting lanterns, greasing wire rigging, making up new halyards and getting through all those other small jobs that make the care of a boat so satisfying an occupation.' He arranged to have her white sails tanned, planned 'a tiny coal stove for people to bark their shins on', and remade the 'dreadful bad splices' left by the other owners. He had originally planned to use *Cochy* as a tender, but Hanson advised him to buy a little pram dinghy; this was christened *Queen Mary*, and when both the Ransomes were aboard, its progress was watched with bated breath.

'Levington brought about a very great change from our home life at Ludderburn,' Ransome wrote in his draft autobiography.

> We were within easy reach of London and I could go up for the day whenever I wanted to chatter, and our friends could run down to chatter with us. Molly Hamilton, Howard of Cape's, my Mother and my Aunt Helen who delighted in going down to the creek and walking along the sea wall watching the ships . . . Pin Mill is the best anchorage on the whole of the East Coast, and when Spring came there were always the little ships of our friends coming in for a day or two before going on elsewhere.

There was one major disappointment. Perhaps miffed at Arthur's temerity at buying *Nancy* on his own, perhaps spoilt by the generously proportioned cabins of *Racundra* and the Broadland hired boats, Evgenia gave *Nancy* the thumbs down. She was too cramped, and her galley – a small Taylor paraffin stove to starboard of the companionway, and a white earthenware 'housemaid' stove for water to port – was impossibly inconvenient.

Evgenia at Broke Farm with her beloved cats Polly and Pudge

THE WORLD OF ARTHUR RANSOME

'Lovely picture of marine happiness': Ransome's sign-off sketch of a storm-rigged *Nancy* on a letter to his mother (4 August 1936)

She announced that she would have nothing to do with her, 'except PERHAPS between May 15th and July 15th'. Twenty years on from their honeymoon, the Terror of the Baltic had become more Susan than Nancy; a cat-loving gardener. Although she did join him on occasion, Ransome often had to look elsewhere for crew. His favourite companion was his Rugby contemporary Philip Rouse, now a naval architect. He and Rouse sailed down to Mersea Island and back in August 1936, 'the best run I've had since coming home to Riga in the gales back in 1922'. They had three reefs in the mainsail, and the storm jib: 'She was quite happy, and fairly flew, big waves picking her up, and she riding the top of them in a flurry of white foam until they passed her and she slipped down to be picked up by the next. It really was gorgeous,' Ransome wrote to his mother. 'Each time I try her under new conditions, I become more and more pleased with her as a sea-boat.'

He lost no time in befriending 'web-footed' young people from other Pin Mill boating families, inviting them into *Nancy*'s cabin to drink ginger pop while they helped with the rigging, and telling them Anansi stories while they painted, varnished and spliced over the winter. 'Supper menu: spaghetti and tomato, salmon and tomato, bananas, hot chocolate and Devonshire cream, thin captain biscuits, butter' ran the log for Taqui's first night afloat. Plum pudding was a year-round staple. He met George and Josephine Russell when they helped him as he came ashore in *Cochy*; the Russells had taken nearby Broke Hall for a year. He taught them to sail, and Josephine was impressed by the fact that he never lost his temper or raised his voice. They helped him moor on their first meeting; this is echoed by the way the Swallows meet Jim Brading in *We Didn't Mean To Go To Sea*. Other families who were frequent companions were the Clays, of *Firefly*, the four 'buccaneering, gun-firing young Youngs', scions of the great brewing family, and the Busks of the 8-ton *Lapwing*, and dinghies *Wizard* and *Zip*.

The Nancy Blackett Trust regularly sails to Holland in Ransome's memory today

that a man can spend months on and in her,' he declared in May, 1937, after 'an extraordinarily pleasant and lucky little cruise' to Portsmouth with Rouse. By then he had got her so well balanced that he could sail her single-handed, and even write while passage-making, 'She would sail by herself without attention while I sat working in cabin or cockpit.'

There are many fairy tales about our failure to realize when we have found our heart's desire. Just as Ransome left the best workroom he had ever had and the country of his heart, so he gave up *Nancy Blackett*, again because of pressure from Evgenia, who had something of the insatiable fisherman's wife of folklore about her. When she wanted to move south in 1935, she had offered the carrot of cruising together again; in January 1938 she told Arthur that if he got a bigger boat, she would take to the ocean wave. How could he resist the prospect of once again commissioning their dream ship? So *Nancy* was sold. In later years, he would kick himself for doing so.

Happily, just as we can roam the Lakes and the Broads in search of Ransome country, so we can sail on his best-loved ship, *Nancy Blackett*, immortalized in *We Didn't Mean to Go To Sea* as *Goblin*. Although she nearly ended up rotting away in Scarborough in the late 1980s, she was saved by Michael Rines, who restored her and then sold her to Colin Winter. In 1996, members of TARS, the Arthur Ransome Society, and other enthusiasts managed to raise £25,000 to buy her, and formed the Nancy Blackett Trust to look after her. She now makes regular appearances at boat shows, and in 2002 she retraced the *Goblin*'s voyage to Flushing (though not in the fog). Going aboard and seeing the sink and the stove, the brass lamps, chronometer and portholes, the four bunks and the capacious store cupboards behind them, you can imagine Ransome in his prime and at his absolute happiest.

Ransome covered over 600 miles in *Nancy* in 1936, generally in shortish trips, with peaceful Kirby Creek on Hamford Water as his favourite destination. '*Nancy* is a good little boat, considering that she was built as a cruiser not a racer and is so comfortable

WE DIDN'T MEAN TO GO TO SEA (1937)

'Here's something to sadden niggards in gold leaf (I name no names),
there are EIGHT words in its entirely admirable memorable and inevitable title . . .
Cheer up. Monosyllables only. But eight of the very best.'
Arthur Ransome, letter to Wren Howard

'During the last four days I have seen, grabbed, clutched and pinioned a really gorgeous idea for another book,' Ransome wrote to Wren Howard on 15 January 1936. 'Swallows only. No Nancy or Peggy or Captain Flint. But a GORGEOUS idea with a first class climax inevitable and handed out on a plate. Lovely new angle of technical approach and everything else I could wish for.' The idea was that the four Swallows, on holiday at Pin Mill, should help an exhausted young man pick up his mooring and tidy up his little ship *Goblin* (a dead ringer for *Nancy Blackett*). Later, he offers to take them for a sail, and they are waiting for him on board when fog descends, the anchor drags, and they find themselves drifting out to sea on their own. Their next stop, after a terrifying night in the North Sea, is Flushing in Holland. The idea evidently owed something to the Clay family, as Ransome dedicated the book to Mrs Henry Clay. They had a son, Jim, who was just about to go up to Oxford, and a cutter called *Firefly*, the same size as *Nancy*, which their children had helmed (though with the parents aboard) on a passage to Holland.

But for the moment, Ransome had to get on with *Pigeon Post*, a task that required iron discipline with his new little ship bobbing at its mooring a short row away, to say nothing of grumbling stomach trouble. On 1 June he had a brief escape to live out the plan of *WDMTGTS* by sailing *Nancy Blackett* across to Holland. His log is full of incidents that provided fine meat for copy, not least the fact that his inexperienced crew stayed seasick below for most of the twenty-four hours it took to reach Flushing;

Ransome at the helm of *Nancy Blackett*

fortunately he succeeded in exchanging him for an efficient young Dutchman for the return voyage.

Once *Pigeon Post* had been despatched, work on the new book could begin in earnest, some of it done during single-handed passages down to Hamford Water, behind Walton-on-the-Naze, where he moored for the night, pottered in the dinghy while he gathered food for thought, and wrote to his heart's content. Much more was achieved, in truth, once *Nancy* was laid up for winter and he was back to the discipline of the workroom. He asked his mother to give him *The North Sea Pilot Part III* for his birthday in January 1937, and the same month he presented copies of *Swallows and Amazons* and *Winter Holiday* to Mrs Powell of Alma Cottage, Pin Mill, 'with a view to preparing her for her appearance in my new book'.

By June he had given a draft to Genia to read and he went off sailing while she did so. 'Flat, not interesting, not amusing', was her verdict. 'Asked if any good chapters? Answer, "No".' There were, it seems, weak points, but it was Molly Hamilton who offered the constructive suggestions that enabled Ransome to revise and finish the book in a way that delighted Cape and even satisfied Genia. It became a tight-knit novel faultlessly driven by the characters of the protagonists – and that of *Nancy* herself. Both its trueness to life ('no room or need for romantic transfiguration of fact', he wrote to Helen Ferris) and its subject matter makes it as much of a handbook for those crossing to Holland as *Racundra* was for sailing the Baltic and *Coot Club* was for a holiday on the Broads.

Ransome was pleased enough with *WDMTGTS* to send it to John Masefield, who wrote to say that he was reading it 'with joy', and praised the pictures. 'You are a lot too modest about your illustrations. All sailors can draw ships; and what could be better than your "Night Encounter" or your tailpieces of the barges and the shag; and the matchless sketch of the salving of the gear at sea.'

ABOVE Anthony Kerins's cover design for the 1967 paperback edition of *We Didn't Mean To Go To Sea*

OPPOSITE, CLOCKWISE FROM TOP LEFT Four of Ransome's drawings for *We Didn't Mean To Go To Sea* (1937): 'All But O.B.', 'Cooking and Steering', 'Night Encounter', 'Rescue at Sea'

SELINA KING (1938–46)

"'But when will she be ready?' asked Nancy.
"Last coat of varnish . . . trifle of rigging . . . another coat to the oars . . .
anchor should be here in the morning . . . You can have her the day after tomorrow.
Better say the day after that.'"

Arthur Ransome, The Picts and The Martyrs

In November 1937, Ransome commissioned Fred Shepherd of Piccadilly, noted for his sturdy cruisers, to design a yacht for them, and Harry King, of Pin Mill, to build her. Evgenia chose the suitably cat-like name *Selina*; *King* was added in honour of Harry's aunt of the same name. She was 34 feet long, with a generous 10-foot beam, a shallow draft well suited to the east coast rivers and a pretty canoe stern. She had a daunting 50-foot mast, but her relatively small mainsail, roller-reefing and double headsails meant that she was easy to sail single-handed if Evgenia preferred to stay below. As well she might. *Selina* had two 6-foot 6-inch settee berths and a cosy coal stove, a writing table, lots of storage space and a spacious and well-fitted galley. Ransome envisaged writing a book about her building, and wrote several chapters of it, describing the pitch pine planks long enough to run her length without a join and oak timbers from ancient local trees planted in the days when their wood was needed for schooners out of Ipswich.

King's began assembling these timbers in March 1938, but had to finish another yacht before they could start work on her. The political skies were darkening, and Ransome began to wonder if he was wise to be building. *Selina* was not finished until late September. Two days later Chamberlain went to parley with Hitler, and returned in triumph announcing 'Peace in our time'. Ransome was less sanguine.

In early October, *Selina*'s lead ballast was loaded, some of it borrowed from another yachtsman's unused store. The Ransomes and Colonel Busk set off down the Orwell and up the Stour for a sail, lunching under way on smoked salmon sandwiches washed down with cider. It was a great success. But their plans to sail to Hamford Water that weekend were spoilt when the owner of the extra ballast took it back. Replacement lead did not arrive until 18 November. Until then, Ransome spent most of his time aboard *Selina*, often sleeping in her, fiddling with small improvements

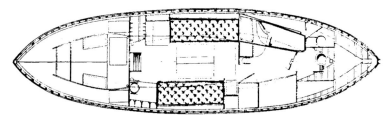

LEFT Interior plan of *Selena King*

OPPOSITE Ransome and Evgenia sailing in *Selena*, towing *Swallow II*

and fishing for eels with sprats, which he stewed on the 'Pongo' stove. Nancy's tender, *Queen Mary*, was replaced with a new, more stable dinghy, yet another *Swallow*.

On 19 November, Arthur and Evgenia set off for a three-hour sail to the Beach End buoy and back. They celebrated with a dinner of duck, peas and potatoes. Next day, they stayed on the mooring, and bad weather forced a second night aboard. It was an exceptionally windy few weeks, and it was only possible to make a few short day trips. But fishing on the mooring won them flounders, dabs, whiting and plaice. 'Came aboard 11.30,' Arthur recorded in the log on 27 December. 'Lit fire. All dry & well. She is a grand ship.'

In January 1939, news came that Harkstead Hall, on the Pin Mill side of the Orwell, was for rent. Flanked with cedars of Lebanon, and standing in a park of its own, it cost £270 a year, plus £25 rates. The Ransomes signed a lease and moved in on 3 April. 'I had a very good room to work in, Genia had a garden in which she did wonders with roses, and Polly and Pudge much preferred it to noisy Levington.' There were still distractions. Ransome asked the headmistress of the local school if the children could play more quietly. Ten years of the deep peace of Low Ludderburn had left him ill equipped for tolerating neighbours of any kind. But he wrote two books there, *Secret Water* and *The Big Six*, and they liked the house so much that they tried to buy it. However, the owner did not want to sell it, even havering about renewing the lease.

Selina was afloat on 6 March, and Ransome's first sail in her was six days later. On 9 April, he sailed for Ipswich with George and Josephine Russell and Jill Busk, but ended up on the mud by the Knoll on a falling tide. George rowed the girls ashore; then there was nothing for it but to wait for the tide to rise again at 4 a.m.

the next day. On 26 April, Arthur set off for Kirby Creek, visited the heronry on Skipper Island and walked across the Wade. The details of *Secret Water* were massing. He and Colonel Busk rowed around in *Swallow* and *Wizard*, and 'took a lot of photographs'. For the next few months, he sailed as often as he could, usually to Kirby Creek. Evgenia came only rarely. 'Mutiny of the crew, vowed never to sail again, but cheered up in the evening,' Arthur wrote on 28 May. She claimed that the galley was 6 inches narrower than it should have been; perhaps she was wider.

War was declared on 3 September 1939. Ransome laid up *Selina* in Oulton Broad for the duration. He would never sail her again. By the time the war was ended, he was over sixty, had ruptured himself twice and was not even allowed to row. He paid her a visit in February 1946, to find her horribly dried out. In March, he agreed to sell her for £1,600, less than she was worth, but saving him the trouble of refitting her.

In early summer 1940, air raids on the military targets of Harwich, Lowestoft and Bawdsey began in earnest. 'The row from the battle here is terrific,' Arthur wrote to his mother on

26 May, the second day of the British Expeditionary Force's fighting retreat and exodus from Dunkirk. He had offered to take *Selina* to Dunkirk, but was told she was too small. 'Poor Genia is getting very little sleep at nights with the row from the aeroplanes and their resisters. The cats, however, are already inured, and merely curse silently out of the corners of their mouths. I go on driving at my infernal book.'

The initial bombardment eased off. In mid-June he went eeling with an old river boatman, which would provide useful copy for *The Big Six*. 'People here are, as I told them they would, getting entirely used to air raids, and trouble about them no more than they would about thunderstorms,' he wrote to Edith on 9 July.

Our beloved Charlie, the farm bailiff, invited me over to see his dugout. He had dug a deep pit and sunk a chicken hut in it, putting logs over the top and a lot of earth. It has a bench in it, and he and his wife and his brother-in-law (Genia's gardener) and his wife all crowd in and play cards by the light of a candle. He

is laying down a little cellar in one corner for the beer he brews himself. I suggested planting nasturtiums overhead, but Charlie very gravely said that he thought them Germs might see 'em, so he is sowing speargrass [asparagus] instead.

By September, however, bombs were a daily hazard. Their sailing friends had left, as had many locals. They were told that they might be told to go at twenty-four hours' notice, taking with them nothing but hand luggage. When someone sent news that an attractive house in Hawkshead was for rent, they began to discuss returning north. On 20 September, Arthur wrote joyfully to his mother that 'Genia says that given a decent house, water supply, indoor sanitation, etc, she is prepared to go back to the Lakes . . . if it does come off, I shall, for one thing at least, be quite grateful to Mr Hitler. It really would be rather lovely to be back in the hills.' He must have driven north almost instantly. A fortnight later he had bought the Heald, a house on Coniston Water. He was heading back to the country of his heart.

SECRET WATER (1939)

'Muddy creeks . . . tidal . . . an island . . . like Walton Backwaters . . .
a hut . . . all hopelessly vague but the business of the islands and the mastodon boy
in his lair on the old barge does seem promising.'

Arthur Ransome, Diary, August 1937

Ransome disliked repeating himself, either in literary form or in plot content, but he was well aware how many of his young fans simply wanted, as one memorable letter put it, 'another book exactly like the last, with the same people, the same places and all the same things happening'. He also had a tendency to be struck by a tempting setting for his next book, often inspired by his immediate surroundings, just as he was mired in the early stages of the one that had to be finished first. While he was writing *Pigeon Post*, he had been buying and sailing *Nancy Blackett*, moving from Low Ludderburn and dreaming of *WDMTGTS*; while he was struggling with *WDMTGTS*, he was overnighting in the Walton Backwaters, mooring in Kirby Creek on Hamford Water, and imagining human eels writhing in the mud, as Daisy, Dum and Dee would in *Secret Water*.

At first he put Dick and Dorothea Callum in; then he replaced them with the Swallows, arranging events so that the story happened in the same summer holiday as *WDMTGTS*. The plot echoed *Robinson Crusoe*. The children are marooned on one of Hamford Water's many islands. They set up camp, live off the land at least a little, and encounter local savages in the shape of the Children of the Eel. Set though it was in his favourite marine playground, *Secret Water* was slow in gestation. *Selina King* was being built and there would again be no new Ransome for Christmas 1938. Instead, new editions of *Swallows and Amazons* and *Swallowdale* appeared with Ransome's own illustrations.

It was observing the Busk family setting up camp on Horsey

Island to chart the backwaters that provided a new direction for the original somewhat formless plot. John, Gillian and Michael Busk become Roger's 'pudding-faces' smartly tying up to *Lapwing*, and then reappeared as the Mastodon Boy's eel-tribe allies Daisy, Dum and Dee, each with a dinghy of their own. Ransome brought George and Josephine Russell to join the camp, and took his usual 'hollywoods'. He began writing in earnest in December. Handling a cast of no fewer than eleven children of ages ranging from five-ish to thirteen or so was made easier by his experience of so many web-footed youngsters both at Pin Mill and on his trips to the Broads as Admiral of the Northern River Pirates. He indulged his love of domestic detail of camp and cabin to the full – the Mastodon's Lair at the end of the barge hulk *Speedy* is one of his most romantic marine homes.

All the woodwork was black with age, and it was a minute or two before they could see what sort of living place this was that the boy had made for himself in the bows of the old wreck. There was a rusty little stove, into which the boy was pushing some scraps of wood. There was a sort of bunk, built into the side with rugs in it. There was a table made of thick black wood, roughly nailed together . . . There was a good solid seat that had clearly once been the thwart of a boat. There were shelves, very rough, along the walls. An old hurricane lantern, not lit, hung from a beam. There were nails driven into the beams, and into the walls, and from these nails hung all kinds of things, fishing lines on wooden winders, a net of some kind, begun but not finished, with a big wooden needle, half full of string, stuck in among the meshes. In one corner were some fishing rods.

There is much gentle comedy in *Secret Water*, and it marked a return from true-to-life adventures to the romanticizing of real surroundings beloved in the Lake books. Published in November, 1939, and dedicated to the Busks, it was also valedictory, finished just as the careless pleasures of sailing at Pin Mill were about to be devastated by a war that would claim the lives of more than one of Ransome's young playmates.

ABOVE Ransome captioned his September 1940 sketch of the Blitz 'Quiet night on the East Coast'
BELOW Ransome's drawing of *Speedy* for *Secret Water* (1939)

THE BIG SIX (1940)

"'Why shouldn't we try to find out for ourselves?" Dorothea went on
almost as if talking to herself. "I've never tried writing a detective story.'"
Arthur Ransome, The Big Six

Although *The Big Six*, Ransome's second book set in the Broads, was written in 1940, it was fictionally set in 1933, the same year as *Coot Club*, and is written as a closely linked sequel. Ransome was thinking hard about how to stop the children growing up, and on a page in his notebook when he was considering a new adventure featuring the Death and Glories, he worked out how he could mesh in their adventures. The Callums never refer in this book to their friends on the Lake in the North, but they must in fact have enjoyed their *Pigeon Post* adventure earlier that summer, and the Swallows' and Amazons' surveying expedition is exploring Secret Water even as the Ds and their Horning allies are hunting for clues in *The Big Six*. Ransome had in fact talked of the idea of a detective story in a January 1938 letter to Margaret Renold, but had laid the idea aside, on Wren Howard's advice, in favour of *Secret Water*.

It says much for the extraordinary elasticity of Ransome's mind that at the age of fifty-six, he chose to experiment with yet another literary form: one invented by his old literary hero, Edgar Allan Poe. He was an avid reader of detective stories, and had been reviewing new ones for the *Observer* under the pen name William Blunt since February 1939, making of the assignments what the late Tim Johns rightly called 'a seminar by a master-storyteller on the art of writing crime stories'. Now he experimented with one of his own, keeping strictly to the 'Rules of the Game' laid down in his very first review for the *Observer*. In this, he said how similar detective stories were to chess problems, and then declared that, if the reader was not to feel cheated, 'there must be only

one possible solution, the pieces must not make moves other than those they could make in the ordinary course of play, and no piece on the board can be an irrelevant idler'.

How far did he succeed? Tom's casting off of the *Margoletta* has been condoned but not forgotten by the Broadland natives, and when boats begin to be cast adrift again, he and the Death and Glories are under suspicion. Crime succeeds crime, all pointing to their guilt. 'What we want are detectives,' says Dorothea, and the six children (Port and Starboard have been sent to school in Paris, as Barbara and Dora had been, twenty years earlier) resolve to become them, establishing Scotland Yard in the Coot Club shed.

Each of Ransome's novels is an education in new skills. *The Big Six* opens with a crude but effective way of removing a loose tooth, and has useful guidance on photography, but it is primarily about pike fishing, which does not merely frame the main plot, the hunt for the villains who are blackening the characters of Pete, Joe and Bill, but plays an integral part. There are lovingly detailed interiors: the magnificent new cabin of the *Death and Glory*, the eel catcher's tarred hulk, Scotland Yard.

The Big Six seems to have almost written itself. Ransome began on New Year's Day 1940, and had finished the first 400-page draft by the end of April. He had not decided on a title. 'I have started full tilt at the revision of *Hot Water, Not Us, Coots in Trouble, Who the Mischief* or God knows what,' he wrote to Wren Howard on May 18. 'Genia said the framework was the best yet, that two of the chapters were good, and that she laughed several times, so I am full of hope.' The anxieties of the political situation were

The background to *The Big Six*: vintage photograph of an eelman's hut, with a wherry

distracting, but he sent the second draft off on 23 July, and set to work on the pictures. The bombing of London that began in September 1940 resulted in the destruction of the first set of blocks, but they were remade in record time, and 12,000 copies were printed in time for Christmas. It is an oddly adult book, somewhat sober, despite the agreeably farcical episodes of the tooth-pulling and meths-drenched Christmas pud (doubtless the latter appealed to Genia). Even as a child, I liked it least of the twelve. But it was the right book for the moment, celebrating traditional country ways and a classic literary form, and featuring the successful conquest of a detestable enemy.

LAKE COUNTRY LANDOWNER
(1940-45)

THE HEALD

'I have emptied my purse, stocking, pockets and mattresses!
Lake frontage in these parts is valued at diamonds an inch.'
Arthur Ransome, letter to Edith Ransome, 1940

The Heald is a veranda-fronted stone bungalow, roofed with green Coniston slate, built in about 1920 halfway between Lanehead and Nibthwaite, close to Fir Island. When Ransome bought it, it had running water, central heating, telephone and electricity. With it came 17 acres of woods and a half-mile of lake frontage, with a small harbour and jetty. 'The actual ground happens to be a bit that I have been in love with since the age of nine. It has a view across the mountains better even than the view from Brantwood.' Ransome also bought the shooting rights to Machell's Coppice, north of his own woods. 'One thing is certain,' he promised Wren Howard. 'It will mean a fresh lot of lake country Swallows and Amazons.'

On 10 October 1940, the Ransomes packed Polly and Pudge into the car and headed northwards via Stamford, where they spent a night at the Haycock Inn, and then Leeds and Settle. 'We crossed the Devil's Bridge over the Lune, and saw once more the Lake hills; I had as always, coming north, the feeling of coming

The Ransomes moved to The Heald, on the east side of
Coniston Water, in October 1940

home.' Evgenia, who had not seen the house, immediately criticized it. The rooms were much smaller than those in their east coast homes, and their furniture and their large selves filled them to capacity. The house was, moreover, almost as remote as Low Ludderburn. Arthur revelled in the peace and the abundant birds and, when *Cochy* arrived from the east coast, fishing on the lake. 'I caught four perch and a minnow just to show it could be done, in our own bay. There is good trout ground all along our half mile.' Evgenia threw herself into fitting blackouts and the impossible task of finding places to put everything. It was not long before she began to complain in earnest, made more grumpy than usual because she was undergoing the menopause. The winter was a cold one, and snow blocked the road in late February. They both caught flu. Sheep invaded the garden – on one memorable occasion Polly the cat, tail erect, herded them away. 'They talk of going to a farm at Blawith for a bit,' Edith wrote to Joyce in July. 'I wish they would. Genia needs a holiday so badly.'

Ransome could not, sadly, run to acquiring the small stone cottage close beside The Heald, which was also for sale, and would

Did Ransome ever work here? Converted to a houseboat after being decommissioned, *Gondola* was moored close to the Heald in the early 1940s

have made an excellent workroom and given them breathing space from each other. It is possible that for a time he rented a houseboat, perhaps even *Gondola*, which was decommissioned in 1938. The children's author Diana Wynne-Jones, who loved Ransome's books, was evacuated to Lanehead with her school during the war. She remembers that one day, some of the mothers took the younger children to the lakeshore to play.

The noise they made disturbed the occupant of the houseboat out in the bay. He came rowing angrily across and ordered them off, and . . . said that he wasn't going to be disturbed by a parcel of evacuees and announced that he would come next morning to complain. He hated children. There was huge dismay among the mothers. Next morning I stood in the hall, watching them rush about trying to find coffee and biscuits (which were nearly unobtainable by then) with which to soothe the great Arthur Ransome, and gathered I was about to set eyes on a real writer.

I watched with great interest as a tubby man with a beard stamped past, obviously in a great fury, and almost immediately stormed away again on finding there was nobody exactly in charge to complain to. I was very impressed to find he was real. Up to then I had thought books were made by machines in the back room of Woolworth's.

Fact or an early instance of the fantasy for which Wynne-Jones was later renowned? Ransome did not have a beard, but he did have a big enough moustache to constitute one in the eyes of an eight-year-old child. He might well have rented a houseboat as a quiet place to work, removed from Evgenia's often explosive discontent.

The summer of 1941 was hot and sunny, and The Heald came into its own. But after fuel rationing began in 1942, life became more difficult; petrol was needed for the electricity generator as well as for driving the 10 miles to Ulverston to shop. Fortunately the butcher delivered, bringing grocery orders as well if they were wanted. Evgenia acquired a little flock of hens, trained to come to the back door to be fed. She ruthlessly executed any that she felt had not earned its portion of the strictly rationed hen food. To economize, and as a back-up to their now elderly car, Ransome acquired a pedal-assisted motorcycle, which he called the Monster. 'I am getting the hang of the animal and yesterday shamelessly took him for a joyride over High Cross and down into Hawkshead and so to High Wray to play chess with Liddell Hart,' he wrote to Charles Renold. 'I got back without trouble, having to pedal only a bit on the worst stretches of those two snorting hills.' He was finding it difficult to get the old-fashioned plus fours that he infinitely preferred to trousers. 'Is there any tailor in Manchester who can COPY a pair of breeches if sent to them?' his letter continued.

Ill health was a recurring problem. Arthur ruptured himself twice, once hauling a shot roe deer through the woods, and again while rowing. After this, he was ordered to row as little as possible. Resourceful to the last, he experimented with fishing for char while sailing. 'The method is that of Bay of Biscay tunny-fishers with mast-high rods travelling under easy sail,' he explained to his mother. 'Last night we had a most luxurious supper on a brace of char, each close on half a pound.'

Annoyances assailed them, tucked away as they were. In summer, the east of lake road was busy with cars full of picnic parties, and some evacuee children vandalized their bay, tearing up water lilies and sinking the dinghy. Evgenia continued to fulminate about her isolation and the weather; she found gardening on rock and in deep shade, with frequent invasions of rabbits, roe deer and sheep, a thankless task. News of the Normandy landings in June 1944 and the likelihood that the war was over meant that they could contemplate moving from The Heald, and Evgenia lost no time in offering the house to a chance acquaintance. Bowing to the inevitable, but also looking forward to the prospect of cruising again, Arthur agreed to sell in a year's time.

Ransome's four and a half years at The Heald were very productive in literary terms, with two books completed (*Missee Lee* and *The Picts and The Martyrs*) and two others embarked upon (*The River Comes First* and *Coots in the North*), to say nothing of early work on *Great Northern?* They were also years of loss. George Russell was killed in action at El Alamein soon after sending his sister a letter full of his plans for sailing with 'Ransie' on his return. John Busk died on HMS *Norfolk* at Scapa Flow. Poor health forced Robin Collingwood to cut short his promising career at Oxford and retire to Coniston, where he died in 1943, after a series of heart attacks, aged only fifty-four. In December 1944, Edith Ransome died, aged eighty-two. Ransome, who was laid low with flu at the time, wrote an intimate and comforting letter to Joyce. 'Remember that all your life you have been the greatest possible pleasure and comfort to her, and that your marriage gave her Hugh as well and then your nice brats in whom she took such pride.'

House-hunting in Suffolk and London filled the first few months of 1945. Evgenia proved hard to please, finding fault with every single Suffolk property they visited, and Arthur was determined, for reasons of marital harmony, that this time the decision should be entirely hers. They had still not found anywhere she liked by 1 June, the agreed date for the sale of The Heald, so they sent the contents of the house into storage in Manchester, and recovered by spending six weeks luxuriating in the Scale Hill Hotel on Loweswater (where Ransome revelled in a room of his own well removed from Genia's). In mid-July, they drove down to London, where they would camp in Jonathan Cape's London flat in Bedford Court Mansions until they found somewhere permanent.

MISSEE LEE (1941)

"Don't hold it in", said Roger. "Let it rip" (advising Nancy on seasickness).'
Arthur Ransome, notebook

The first book that Ransome wrote at the Heald was, despite his promise that the move would mean lots more Lake books, another fantasy yarn in the mould of *Peter Duck*. Cape felt that something escapist would comfort children confused by the upheavals of war. Ransome, who had considered just such a book before embarking on *Secret Water*, rose to the occasion superbly, with *Wild Cat* catching fire while the Swallows and Amazons are on a voyage round the world in her with Captain Flint. 'Motto for the whole book: Let it Rip!' was the heading for his first notes on the story, at that stage called *Poor Miss Lee*, but he never used the promising incident in which Roger advises Nancy on seasickness. He faltered in the early stages, asking the Renolds for ideas, and they came up with one involving evacuees. Cape disagreed: the new story was to avoid the war completely.

What got the tale going again was Evgenia's idea that he should set the shipwreck of the *Wild Cat* off the coast of China. This enabled him to use his own experience there in 1926–7 to the full; the colourful dragon processions and unusual ways of fishing were all faithfully reproduced. Nancy meets a real she-pirate in the shape of Cambridge-educated Missee Lee, who is a happy combination of the elegant Madame Sun Yat Sen, who had been educated at Wesleyan College, Georgia (his original notes have his she-pirate graduating from an American university), a Chinese girl who had indeed been educated at Newnham in the 1930s, and Lai Choi San, a 'female sea robber' of whom Ransome had read in his copy of Aleko E. Lilius' *I Sailed With Chinese Pirates* (1930). It was far from unusual for women to handle boats in the China of the time, and several of them were successful warlords in their own right. The organized protection racket run by the warlords was also true to life, though Ransome watered down his pungent pronouncements on

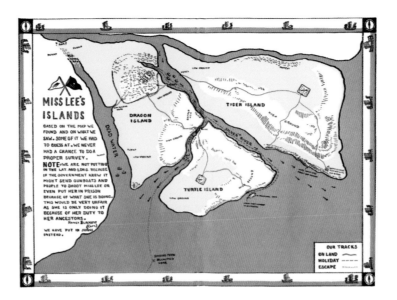

them in his notebooks: 'Wellington Koo – the most detestable little worm I have ever seen. Oily with a weak, cruel, uncertain scratch of a mouth, swollen heels to his jaws, wide eyes well practised in lack of expression, a poisonous little maggot of a man.'

The feeling description of the discomfort of riding donkeys recalled Moab at Hatch; Roger's unexpected flair for Latin, which saves all their lives, derived from Ransome's own schooldays sweating over Kennedy's *Latin Primer*. The whole crew effects a daring escape by skipping away under their very own dragon and boarding the graceful junk *Shining Moon*, leaving a sad Miss Lee to observe the duty a child owes a parent in true Confucian style. As Ransome wrote of her successful career at Newnham, he may also have been wondering what would have happened if he had accepted W. D. Rouse's offer to coach him for Oxford entrance instead of observing the duty he felt he owed to his family by opting to study science in Leeds at the age of sixteen.

There are many ways in which *Missee Lee* was relevant to 1940 rather than escapist. The sinking of *Wild Cat* was a symbol of the many Allied ships being sunk. Ransome had effectively lost his own ship. He had sadly tucked *Selina* up in Oulton Broad, and

OPPOSITE Ransome's photo of a Chinese island was copied (right) by Edith Ransome to help him with a drawing for *Missee Lee* (1941)

ABOVE LEFT Madame Sun Yat Sen was part of the inspiration for *Missee Lee*
ABOVE RIGHT Ransome's endpaper map for *Missee Lee*

was already regretting *Nancy*. Like everyone else in wartime, the shipwrecked crew of *Wild Cat* have to eke out rations, carefully assessing how to make them last. And the dangerous prospect of an alliance of Tiger Island and Turtle Island against Dragon Island mirrored that of the Russian–German pact.

Miraculously, Evgenia was restrained in her criticisms, and since the book's excellent and vivid scaffolding contained a well-thought-out plot, there was no stopping progress. On 18 September 1941 Wren Howard telegraphed Ransome: 'FINISHED PROOFS MIDNIGHT STOP CONGRATULATIONS TWENTY TWO GONG STORY', and then wrote to say, 'I have honestly enjoyed reading every word of the book and finding such a crop of Ransome subtleties.' Despite wartime paper shortages, 20,500 copies of *Missee Lee* were published on 5 December 1941. 'Mr Ransome's zest and power of invention seem inexhaustible,' wrote a reviewer in the *Yorkshire Post*.

THE PICTS AND THE MARTYRS:
OR, NOT WELCOME AT ALL (1943)

'She turned to look at the Dogs' Home that was now to be a house for Picts. Were they really going to live in that old hut, alone, high in the wood, with no one else within sight or call? Were they going this very night to sleep in it, and wake in it tomorrow alone and secret, like escaping prisoners hiding in a hostile country?'

Arthur Ransome, The Picts and The Martyrs

The Picts and The Martyrs was the first Ransome book to be set in the Lakes for seven years, but he arranged the timings of the intervening books so ingeniously that the children have aged hardly at all. The adventure is set in the summer after that bumper Ransome Time year in which no fewer than five adventures took place, and so the Ds and the Amazons are meeting for the first time since *Pigeon Post*. Ransome is careful to point this out in the opening chapter. 'For nearly a year they had not been in the north,' the Ds reflect as they cross the lake in *Amazon*, gazing at High Topps, where they fought a fell fire during the last summer's drought, and High Greenland, where they made an expedition across the frozen lake to the North Pole in the exceptionally cold winter before it. Cook is telling them how they have grown since the year before, when the homing pigeons' alarm bell startles her into dropping plates, and Colonel Jolys' card 'IN CASE OF FIRE RING FELLSIDE 75' is still propped up by the telephone.

The Ds' brand-new dinghy *Scarab* (recognizably *Cochy*) is about to leave the boatyard for the Beckfoot boathouse, and the plan is for a fortnight of learning to sail in her under Captain Nancy's tuition until the Swallows arrive at Holly Howe. Cook will hold the fort, Nancy will learn to housekeep, and their old friend Squashy Hat, who is living on the houseboat while checking assays from the new copper mine, will look in on Beckfoot every other day. But there are to be no 'wildnesses' until Mrs Blackett, who had been

taken on a Nordic cruise by Captain Flint to recover from a severe bout of flu, returns. 'I don't know what Aunt Maria would say if she knew I was leaving you alone,' she says on her departure. This throwaway line proves to be an unexploded bomb. No sooner have the Ds arrived than a letter from Great-Aunt Maria does the same, announcing that, appalled to hear that they are on their own, she is coming to look after Nancy and Peggy.

Convinced that she would be even more incensed if she knew that they had friends staying, the Amazons decide to conceal the Ds in a small hut in the woods known as the Dogs' Home. 'What her codfish eyes don't see, her conger heart won't grieve over,' announces Nancy, still something of an Eel. There is much domestic detail on settling in, and local lad Jacky to help them live 'like badgers', showing them how to tickle trout and cook rabbits caught in the woods: all things that Ransome was revelling in doing himself. Of course Great-Aunt Maria gets suspicious, especially when Dick creeps into the house for essential equipment from Uncle Jim's study for Squashy Hat's work. How she gets her comeuppance involves ingenious plotting, driven, as Ransome always liked it to be, by the character of the protagonists. 'I don't know how other people make plots,' he wrote to his Aunt Helen (to whom he dedicated the book). 'It is my slow and painful method, checking events by characters, and expecting the characters, by being themselves, to produce the events.'

A tumbledown stone hut in Machell's Coppice, near the Heald (left), closely resembles Ransome's drawing of the 'Dogs' Home' (right), Dick and Dorothea's hideout in *The Picts and The Martyrs* (1943)

There is something heartfelt in Ransome's invention of the Dogs' Home, especially as there is just such a retreat a short distance from the Heald. He must often have sat in it, watching birds and smoking in blessed seclusion, while he thought out the practical details of living there, safely removed from an overbearing and opinionated woman: hammocks slung from the old wooden pegs in its beams, a little dam in the stream to make a washing pool, a jampot with wild flowers in it. That was the easy bit, all written in the first three months of 1942. The dénouement was slow in coming, and by March he was despairing. 'I wish I had another wild *Peter Duck* or *Missee Lee* plot. The new book with its strictly domestic interest is damnable. I hate it and so will everyone else.' One problem was that he had no sounding boards, no eager young listeners for him to read aloud to, only his 'Critic on the Hearth'. Evgenia was dead set against the book. She wrote a searing letter to Arthur, who was taking cover in London while she was reading the finished typescript, warning him that it was 'too grown-up and facetious for a children's book', and would ruin his reputation for all time. Crushed, he accepted her opinion and did not send it to Cape. 'I feel as if with much thought and trouble I had built

a motor car, and painted and varnished all pretty, only to find it wouldn't move and never could,' he wrote to Margaret Renold.

After a few months of misery during which he considered different subjects, the worm turned. Without Genia knowing, Arthur made some revisions, and sent it to his mother. She expressed enthusiasm, and he resolved to let Cape, who had loved it from the start, have it in November. 'The book cannot and must not be mentioned again in this house,' Ransome wrote warningly to his mother on 29 December. As a wry joke, he subtitled it *Or, Not Welcome At All*. It was, of course, too late for it to appear for Christmas, but when it was published in June 1943, it sold over 22,000 copies in six months – something of a miracle considering how little actually happens in it, but less of one considering the fact that, as he wrote in a letter to the Renolds while he was struggling with *Missee Lee*, 'at least seven in ten of my infant correspondents write demanding another S and A with the lake background'.

THE MIGHT-HAVE-BEENS

"'Grab a chance, and you won't be sorry for a might-have-been.'"
Commander Ted Walker, RN, in Arthur Ransome, We Didn't Mean To Go To Sea

Fishing preoccupied Ransome after his return to the Lake Country

Ransome began but never finished two other books. *The River Comes First* was to have been an historical novel about the Bela, his favourite Lakeland fishing river, as it was of his father and his grandfather before him. On its banks, he met Tom Stainton, happily growing old in his job as 'beck-watcher' to the Bela; he had been appointed in Tom Ransome's time, and remembered Cyril well. He began to map out a rural adventure set in Victorian times, and centring on the efforts of 'Tom Staunton' to catch a gang of commercial poachers who are greedily set on blasting the life out of the river. Around this core, Ransome spun an evocative web of landscape, wildlife and fishing lore worthy of Isaac Walton. He started work in November 1942. Six chapters, some 28,000 words, were finished by May 1943. They make fine reading, as do some surviving first-person episodes, notably one on poachers' unsporting ways, and a heart-stopping account of the rescue of Tom's playmate Jenny from an island in the river when a cloudburst threatens to swamp it and them. If he had managed to complete the book, it would have been a classic of nature writing.

It was not to be. For whatever reason, and one cannot help thinking of a 6-foot-tall one full of caustic opinion, he gave up the river book, and began to plan a new children's adventure, *Swallows & Co.* The last page of *The Picts and The Martyrs* flagged this up. 'Now at last we're free to start stirring things up again,' exclaims Nancy. 'We'll hoist the skull and crossbones again the moment we've had our grub. We'll get things moving without wasting a minute.' It may have been the prospect of heading south in a year's time that made him think of re-introducing Joe, Bill and Pete, the three junior members of the Coot Club. But since he had one more year in the north, why not bring them up there as fresh eyes through which to conjure up the familiar territory of Rio, Dixon's Farm and Wild Cat Island?

The draft of the book begins with Joe, Pete and Bill in Horning, watching hordes of hullabaloos competing for moorings. There is no room at the Swan, so they tie up at Jonnatt's boatyard. There they see a newly finished cruiser being loaded on to a lorry, and discover that she is going to the very Lake in the North beside which Dick and Dorothea are holidaying. '"Pity you can't make the voyage in her,"' says Mrs Barrable, when she hears where *Bonnka* is going, and walks on 'without looking back, like one who has dropped a stone in a pool but does not wait to see where the ripples go. Joe was struck suddenly silent.'

Go they do, stowing away in the well-appointed cabin of the cruiser, with Joe's white rat ('couldn't leave him behind'). Ransome's narrative ends at this point, and he had several possible continuations. One had the three boys leaving the boat only to see it and the lorry speeding away from them. They race after it, seeing the lake 'and two white sails waiting for a breath of wind. "Talk about Wroxham Broad," gasped Pete. "That beat Breydon," said Bill.'

They find the cruiser, already launched. A light goes on in its window and through it they see *Bonnka*'s new owner sitting on one of the bunks. 'And on the table was Joe's white rat, eating bread and milk out of a saucer.' *Bonnka*'s owner takes pity on them. The only other chapter has the boys experiencing the lake, the houseboat with its elephant flag and Wild Cat Island flying a huge Jolly Roger. As they row from *Bonnka* to Dixon's Farm, they see three small boats, two expertly sailed, one (the Ds in *Scarab*) distinctly uncertain, coming out from behind the island. A long thin boat rowed by a stout, bald-headed man is approaching from the houseboat. One of the dinghies has capsized. '"Salvage!"' shouts Joe. His attempt to rescue what he thinks is a drowning

Ransome's sketch of the interior of *Bonnka*, the Broads cruiser in which the Death and Glories hitch a ride north in the unfinished Swallows and Amazons adventure *Swallows & Co*, also known as *Coots in the North*

girl is rewarded by a resounding blow to his head. '"Shiver my timbers!" said an angry voice. "What are you playing at? Tearing my hair out by the roots. Hullo! Did I get your nose? Good."'

There are copious notes concerning what happens next, visions splendid of a fleet of dinghies fishing for char under sail, inspired by a postcard of Bay of Biscay tunny-fishers which Pete finds on Captain Flint's houseboat. Another episode has the houseboat going adrift in a gale, and the Death and Glories going into salvage mode with the help of *Bonnka*. But Ransome never finished it. He turned back again to *The River Comes First*, but that did not move forward either. Those interested in reading what survives of both books can turn to Hugh Brogan's edited versions of them and other fragments in what he called *Coots in the North* (1988).

THE YO-YO YEARS
(1945–67)

PETER DUCK (1945–8)

*'She will be P.D. among friends. A comic little boat with two masts, so as to keep each
single sail small and light to handle. She'll sleep two in comparative comfort.'*
Arthur Ransome, letter to Charles Renold, 9 November 1945

After leaving the Heald in 1945, the Ransomes veered uncertainly between the civilized comforts of London with the option of cruising on the south coast and the siren call of the solitude of the Lakes. As the headings in this section suggest, when in London, boats took precedence; when in the Lakes, the house. And there was one more book about the Swallows, Amazons and Ds to come. Before they left the Heald, Arthur had received a letter outlining a plot that he quickly realized would be their ideal twelfth and last adventure. But although he had begun work on what would become *Great Northern?*, he was much more interested in the progress of his new boat.

His doctors voted *Selina* too large for safety, so he sold her, and asked Laurent Giles to design a 'ketch-rigged bathchair' for him, and Harry King to build it at Pin Mill. As usual, he took much pleasure in specifying internal comforts: a chest of drawers, a niche for a writing bureau, plenty of headroom. In August 1946, he went down to Pin Mill to check progress on *Peter Duck*, as Giles

View from Uig Lodge, Isle of Lewis, the setting for *Great Northern?*

had christened her – just the name for an Ancient's boat. When he cracked his head as he sat down on the fore end of his bunk, he began to have reservations. Evgenia did too, but they decided that they should at least try her out. Early in October 1946, they had a pleasant cruise in her with Colonel Busk, who voted her cabin roomy and comfortable. The Ransomes disagreed, and sold her back to Giles. A month later, they had second thoughts, but had to pay an extra £300 to buy her back.

In April 1947, Arthur set sail in *Peter Duck* from Burnham-on-Crouch, in convoy with Busk in his own new yacht, *Maid Meriel*. The wives cautiously followed on land, staying at hotels. The cruise was plagued by particularly wet weather, engine faults, leaks in the cabin roof and the failure of the winch – a disaster considering Ransome's tendency to ruptures. The bunks were much too narrow, as cushion backs had been fitted against his wishes, and since the leaks proved stubborn, the bedding was soaked. Worse, the Pin Mill harbour-master failed to find him a decent mooring.

But *Peter Duck* sailed well, and when the glitches were finally sorted, even Evgenia expressed qualified enthusiasm. When she

sailed with Arthur on one tricky passage, he noted in his log, 'Cook promoted to mate.'

In September, they abandoned Pin Mill for West Mersea, on the Crouch, 'a v. good place for small sailing boats . . . nearer than Lowestoft or Walton, and much nicer than Burnham'. Colonel Busk moved *Maid Meriel* there too. They joined the yacht club, and had a fortnight of almost daily cruises. There were more excellent cruises in late August and September, on one occasion 'hogging 2 BRICKS of Walls ice-cream with a tot of rum' at the yacht club.

Domestically, life was less satisfactory. Evgenia had finally settled on a spacious first-floor flat in Weymouth Street, London, close both to Cape and to Arthur's doctor in Harley Street. At first, all was well. Ransome wrote to Margaret Renold on 14 October 1945 that 'Genia swears that once we are straight she will be able to take things much easier than in any of our earlier camps.' It was an all too accurate description of their frequently changed homes. 'I must admit that my big workroom is really a very good one', he went on, 'and even at my advanced age (at which imagination cools and no sort of inspiration can be hoped

for) I ought to be able to turn out some sort of substitute for decent books. And hot water day and night is a bit of a blessing.' He brought *Cochy* down from Coniston to sail on the river at Tamesis, the historic Hampton sailing club. He was also close to Broadcasting House, and enjoyed discussing the adaptation of *Swallows and Amazons* for 'Uncle Mac' to read on *Children's Hour*. He went to Twickenham to watch rugby with Rupert Hart-Davis. 'I'm not going to hate it as much as I thought I should,' he wrote to Liddell Hart. Weymouth Street was certainly a good place to see out the ferociously cold winter of 1946/7.

But noise from the now omnipresent wirelesses assailed them on all sides – as it inevitably must in a flat. In January 1948, they began to look again for a rural home, possibly in West Mersea, where the Busks had settled, or the Berkshire Downs, near their many friends with fishing rights on the trout streams of the south. But towards the end of the month they went to view several properties in the Lake Country. Arthur found one of them irresistible. Contracts for Lowick Hall, in the heart of the countryside of his boyhood holidays, were signed on 5 April.

What of *Peter Duck*? The last day of January 1948 found

Arthur painting and varnishing her, and making some small improvements. The galley was widened so that it could take a two-burner stove. Lunch was two dozen freshly harvested oysters. But house-hunting and moving north meant that there was no sailing to speak of that year, and the theft of the lead ballast, then very hard to replace, over the winter, prevented it in 1949. In October 1949 *Peter Duck* was sold. In 1957, she was bought by George Jones, a yacht agent who suggested that Laurent Giles built more. Thirty-eight were launched between 1960 and 1970. The Jones family loved the original. 'She's a sea-kindly little boat,' Mrs Jones told me when I was researching *Captain Flint's Trunk* in 1984. 'I sometimes think we ought to sell her, but I can never quite bear to part with her.' She was sold in 1987 to Greg and Ann Palmer, and had a decade of adventurous sailing, even going to St Petersburg. After Greg Palmer's untimely death in 1997, *Peter Duck* was bought back into the Jones family by Julia Jones, who has never forgotten her childhood experiences sailing in her. Julia is an Amazon after Ransome's own heart, and is now writing a series of books aimed at today's web-footed youngsters.

GREAT NORTHERN? (1947)

""What's hit's history: what's missed's mystery.'"
Mr Jemmerling, in Arthur Ransome, Great Northern?

The origins of *Great Northern?* were deliberately shrouded in mystery: Genia mendaciously referred to early fishing trips to the Hebrides to explain its genesis to Hugh Brogan. It was only when I was trawling through letters to Ransome in the Brotherton Library that its true history emerged. Myles North, the son of Lake Country friends of Arthur and Evgenia, had grown up with Ransome's books, and was an expert on birds and wildlife and a sailor. He was in Somaliland while in the East African Colonial Service when he answered an invitation passed on by his mother to go sailing with Arthur after the war was over. 'I have enjoyed your books tremendously,' he wrote on 22 June 1944.

> I like the people you write about, and their quite remarkable 'aliveness' and characterisation. Given any set of circumstances, the reader knows just how Nancy or Roger or Susan would feel . . . I'd be inclined to compare your way with Buchan's and Conan Doyle's, both of whom to my mind do it very simply and with great charm . . . Your parts about sailing and seamanship give me the greatest pleasure, and my goodness, it's practical! This line is your forte of course, but the motif of practicality runs through all your stories and is one of their greatest charms. Everything works.

It must have been immensely cheering for Ransome, at a time when he was feeling deeply bruised by Genia's lack of enthusiasm for his work, to hear from someone who grasped exactly what he was so skilfully achieving. He read on, and found a detailed outline headed 'Suggested Great Northern Diver Story'. The central idea was the rarity of Great Northern Divers in the British Isles. 'Any egg collector would sell his soul for the first British-taken eggs of the Great Northern Diver.' The plot had Captain Flint sailing in the Hebrides (which North knew well, though Ransome did not) with the Swallows, Amazons and Ds in *Wild Cat* (North must have missed out on *Missee Lee*). They land to scrape barnacles off the bottom of their boat, and meet an egg-collector, whom Dick, long a keen ornithologist, is prepared to worship – until he discovers that Mr Jemmerling shoots birds not with a camera but with a gun. Then it is a race against time and a horde of angry Gaels to save the lives and eggs of the pair of Great Northern Divers that Dick has discovered on an island in a little loch.

Ransome abandoned *Swallows & Co*, and began to embellish North's scenario. He read *Log of the Blue Dragon*, C. C. Lynam's 1910 account of a family cruise around the Hebrides, and Osgood Mackenzie's *Hundred Years of Life in the Highlands* (1921), which produced a blind piper and a peppery laird. He substituted *Sea Bear*, a Norwegian pilot vessel borrowed from Erling Tambs' 1933 *Cruise of the Teddy*, for *Wild Cat*, and started Dorothea on a 'Romance of the Hebrides'. He had written 280 pages by Christmas 1944, but was far from happy with it, not least because he did not know the setting. 'Awfully dull stuff.' He wrote to the Renolds: 'You can feel my immobility of head in every line of it. But perhaps just as well, because it will make it less heart-rending to pull it to pieces and rewrite it after getting a squint at the Hebrides to check the details, which are probably all wrong.'

The Ransomes went to the Isle of Lewis in mid-May 1945, staying in a Stornoway hotel. Arthur later regaled the Garrick Club with the tale of how he set off to fish one day with his customary lunch, a package containing a bottle of milk and a packet of biscuits prepared by the hotel. When he settled down to eat it he found that he had been given the package intended for a party of local celebrities: a bottle of whisky, then all but unobtainable.

There was little progress on the book in 1945. Ransome was preoccupied with settling in to London and talking to Laurent Giles about the design of *Peter Duck*. He also took a fishing holiday on the Broads in September. He was finding the long haul of a novel harder and harder work. By February 1946 he had sent a draft to Wren Howard, and was given some useful criticism. He and Genia visited the Hebrides again in June, the season in which

Arthur had decided to set the story, as he wanted the pregnancy of the hinds to be the reason for the old laird's fury at the invasion of his land by children. They stayed with the Dobsons at Uig Lodge, recognizably the Castle of the Gaels and now a comfortable hotel. The book was finished early in January 1947. Cape printed 44,500 copies for its August publication, rightly thinking that there would be a huge demand for the first Ransome book for four years. It was also the last, something that Ransome consciously or not seems to have been aware of, affectionately referring to earlier adventures in it, but making it clear that the oldest children at least are all but grown up. There is no celebratory Highland feast at the end, no promise of adventures to come, just the Young Gael watching a little ship disappearing towards the horizon. The birds have flown.

LOWICK HALL (1948–50)

'Crumbling plaster, dust, bad drains, decrepit water-pipes, rotting floors,
leaking roofs, etc. But Golly what a place!'

Arthur Ransome, letter to Joyce Lupton, 1948

'I feel a little like Sir Walter Scott,' quipped Arthur Ransome in a letter to Joyce after he and Evgenia moved into Lowick Hall, an ancient house halfway between Nibthwaite and Greenodd, and ten minutes' walk from the Crake. Heavy with history, the steading had been held by the Norman knight Ivo de Taillebois in the 1080s, and his pele tower was still the core of the house. Its oldest rooms and its oak staircase dated from the sixteenth century. Most of Lowick dated from the 1740s, but its Victorian owners had put in generous windows and a substantial porch. It had been neglected for two decades, and lacked bathrooms, electricity and telephone.

An army of workmen moved in after they acquired it on 6 April 1948. There was still only one habitable room when they arrived early in June. Ransome wrote to Joyce:

The rhododendrons are gorgeous from where I am writing, and from the garden there is the most beautiful view of the Old Man I have ever found . . . WHEN all the plasterers and painters and plumbers and whatnots are gone, the place will be really quiet, and I ought to be able to get on with some writing to pay for it all!!! Chickens laying well! Mice by the thousand. Genia seems quite undismayed and sees the vision of the house as it is to be gleaming before her all the time.

The Ransomes moved to Lowick Hall, near Greenodd, in 1948

They escaped to the Isle of Lewis for three weeks in July, staying with the Dobsons again. Fishing was now Ransome's greatest pleasure in life. 'The fisherman's body may be sitting at a table in a lamplit room but he is far away, listening to the splash and tumble at the weir, noting the dimple of a trout on a smooth run between weedbeds, feeling his heart quicken at the stir of a salmon,' he wrote in *Fishing*, the last but one of his books. Fishing was certainly a large part of the attraction of Lowick. He was cock-a-hoop to have been elected a member of the Leven Angling Association in March 1949, 'about the best mixed fishing in the north of England, brown trout, sea-trout and salmon, all within reasonable reach'.

Arthur enjoyed playing at Lord of the Manor, and it was good to be near the Kelsalls and the Gnossies once again. But the house and its grounds were a challenge to manage; he was now in his mid-sixties, and Genia a far from fit fifty-five-year-old. In the spring of 1949 both their gardener and their charwoman gave notice. Genia was notoriously impatient with domestic help, and it proved difficult to find replacements. Arthur had a severe attack of shingles, and took months to recover. Although Lowick was less remote than the Heald, it was very isolated. But it was, as Arthur had hoped, a very pleasant place in which to write. He was working, 'in spite of strong local opposition', on a translation of a French book of West African folk tales. Again, Genia's disapproval made him lose confidence in the project. Instead, he began work on his autobiography, a model of the genre, and one of the most attractive of all the books he wrote for adults.

Another enjoyable occupation was advising Rupert Hart-Davis on books to publish. Rupert Hart-Davis had left Cape in 1946 to set up his own publishing imprint. Wanting to publish a classic of sail, he asked Ransome about Joshua Slocum's *Sailing Alone Around the World*. 'The best sailing book in the world,' Ransome replied. 'And if you publish it I'll write you an introduction for

Ransome in his favourite clothes:
tweed jacket and plus fours

nothing.' The book sold so well that Hart-Davis made it the first in a 'Mariners Library'. Would Ransome be 'godfather and nanny' to the series? Ransome came up with ideas galore. Forty-eight books were published in all, including *Racundra's First Cruise*. Between 1948 and 1954, Ransome introduced seven of them. The ones he chose were by independent-minded eccentrics after his own heart.

The first after Slocum was the Norwegian Erling Tambs's *The Cruise of the Teddy*. Ransome had reviewed this book about a family voyage every bit as thrilling as *WDMTGTS* when it came out in 1933, and used the *Teddy* as a model for *Sea Bear* in *Great Northern?* Next came McMullen's *Down Channel* (1901), a book which had informed *Peter Duck*. Ransome adapted his introduction for an earlier reprint, adding new material on the design of McMullen's boats. Then came two by E. F. Knight, whose handbook *Sailing* accompanies John on the *Goblin*. Knight's *Falcon on the Baltic*,

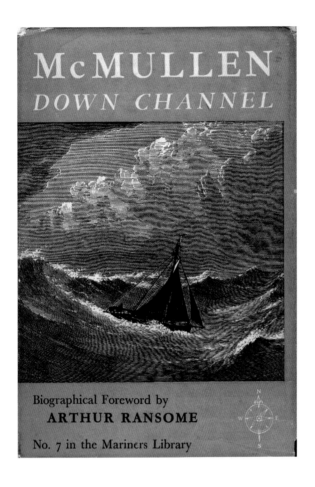

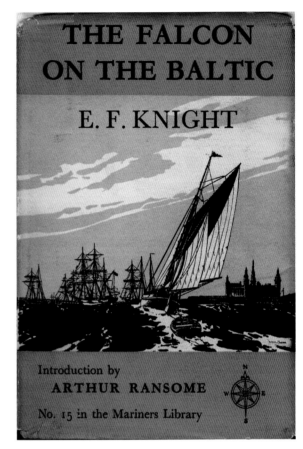

written in 1888, was the model for *Racundra's First Cruise*. 'At 3 am, June 22nd, I put the needful stores into the dinghy, the eggs (half a dozen, hard-boiled), bread, cheese, a bottle of rum and water, pipes, matches, and plenty of tobacco, a sketch-book and a compass, and I did not forget to take a blanket in case I was benighted and had to sleep out' could as easily have been written by Ransome as by Knight. The second Knight was *The Cruise of the Alerte* (1890), which had also provided ideas for *Peter Duck*. *The Cruise of the Kate* (1880) by E. E. Middleton is the tale of the author's circumnavigation of Great Britain in a 25-foot rowing boat. Ransome's final choice was by the man who had inspired Knight and Middleton, John MacGregor. *The Voyage Alone in the Yawl Rob Roy* (1867) is a stirring account of building a 21-foot-

long boat in London, filling it with Protestant tracts, and sailing it to Napoleon III's Paris Exhibition to convert the papist French.

The high point of Ransome's time at Lowick was the arrival in June 1949 of the twelve-volume *Oxford English Dictionary* as a thank-you from Rupert Hart-Davis.

IT has arrived. We are planning to move to a larger house to make room for IT. When the new part of Lowick was built in 1748, no-one foresaw that it would have to house a *Great Oxford English Dictionary*. Not one of my hats will fit my head as I go prancing around, the owner of a *Great Oxford English Dictionary* . . .

IT has the most extraordinary effect upon me. Looking

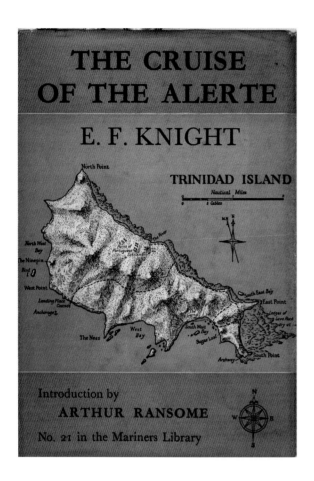

In the late 1940s and early 1950s, Ransome was 'godfather and nanny' to Rupert Hart-Davis's Mariners Library series

at IT full face, or even feeling ITS blue buckram presence warming my back, I have the oddest illusion that after all I must be some sort of a writer.

I daren't risk the loss of that illusion by trying to write.

He housed it nobly in a glass-fronted cupboard installed in Lowick Hall in 1748, and carved with the arms of the Blencowes, the house's then owners.

After only two years, the Ransomes decided that Lowick was too much for them. Arthur had expressed his doubts as to their managing as early as March 1949; by June, Genia agreed with him. In October 1950, they sold, at a heavy loss, and moved back to London.

LOTTIE BLOSSOM (1952–5)

*'Nothing can be brought into this world without labour and pain, but that is soon
lost sight of, and in its place comes the pleasure of seeing the thing we have created
living its life, and it is because of this latter fact that the human race will continue,
and owners will continue to build their own yachts.'*

Uffa Fox, Thoughts on Yachts and Yachting

Hurlingham Court is a block of spacious mansion flats built in the 1890s, facing Ranelagh Gardens, in Fulham. Flats at the back have a glorious view of the Thames near Putney Bridge. In 1950 the Ransomes bought number 40, on the fourth floor, and retained it for the next thirteen years, making it the home that they owned longest of all. The flat struck early visitors as hideously furnished. Over the years it became comfortably lined with rich memories of the past, tributes in the shape of models of boats, real and china cats, and of course books. An Audubon print of an Arctic Tern had pride of place, as did a stuffed perch arranged in front of a

In 1950, the Ransomes moved to 40 Hurlingham Court, a two-storey flat overlooking the Thames at Fulham

bright green bank of reeds, and a photograph of John Masefield, then Poet Laureate. Ransome enjoyed slipping back into his habit of dropping into the Garrick to play chess and billiards, for lunch, and even for dinner on occasions when Genia did not want to feed him at home.

To compensate for leaving the Lakes, Genia had agreed that she and Arthur should buy a new boat. They liked the look of a 27-foot Hillyard 6-tonner, sloop-rigged, with a central cockpit and wheel steering, but began cautiously by chartering *Barnacle Goose*, a similar boat. They had 'a very lazy carpet-slippered cruise', the epitome of domesticity afloat. With like-minded friends they planned a Force 1–2 Cruising Club, with a pair of carpet slippers on its burgee. They then ordered a 27-foot Hillyard sloop for £1,300. She was to have tanned sails and a canoe stern. Genia decided to call her *Lottie Blossom*, after her favourite P. G. Wodehouse character.

Their first voyage was on 19 April 1952. They left Littlehampton in West Sussex at 5 a.m., and reached Itchenor at 10 a.m. They explored Chichester Harbour, and then a horrendous gale kept them on their mooring for two days. A few days later, the cruise was cut short when Ransome was seized with agonizing stomach pains, and had to be rushed to hospital for an operation on his prostate gland. He was unable to sail for three weeks. They set off again late in June, but Arthur's ulcer began to play up, and towards the end of July, he had to summon his doctor again.

Ransome and Evgenia at Hillyard's Littlehampton boatyard, where they acquired *Lottie Blossom* in 1952

The second *Lottie Blossom* under sail in 1954

Undeterred, they set sail again, sensibly with two strong young men as crew, and had some fine sailing, rejoicing in overtaking some bigger yachts.

They discovered the attractions of the Hamble River at Bursledon in Hampshire, and socialized agreeably with other boats. Then they moved across to the Beaulieu River, and were given a quiet mooring a little above the bustle of Buckler's Hard. 'Lovely quiet night, and in the early morning pheasants, curlews and woodpigeons.' Genia went mushroom-picking and cooked them for supper. After returning to the Hamble, they motored up the Emsworth Channel, exploring Thorney and Bosham, where they found *Racundra* on a mud berth. 'Hull looking much the same, a very good intelligent hull, but now she has some sort of silly doghouse, and, of course, years ago an earlier owner had

cut the great beam that carried the bridge deck.' They got back to Littlehampton on 12 September.

For all the good times they had had that season, they had found the centre cockpit too small; Genia disliked floundering under the mainsail when it descended. They asked Hillyard to build a new version of his design in which the aft cabin was scrapped, making the main one palatial; a third berth was tucked into the fo'castle in case a crew was required. They found a buyer who paid what they had for the original *Lottie*, and was happy to change her name to his own favourite: she became *Ragged Robin III*, and is now owned by Ted and Diana Evans.

When they sat in the new *Lottie* at the end of January 1954, Arthur noted that 'the cabin is colossal. If we are not comfortable in this boat, we ought to be.' *Lottie* was not ready to sail when they had hoped to, on 11 April, Genia's birthday, but once she was afloat and seaworthy, they had their best ever summer of cruising. Ransome found he could write comfortably in the new cabin, and worked on his last Mariners Library introduction, to MacGregor's *Voyage in the Yawl Rob Roy*. They spent over thirty days afloat, this time going properly foreign. They sailed to Cherbourg on 26 and 27 July, had a sociable week in port, and then sailed home, in a gale and with no engine, on 6 August. It took nineteen hours, for eighteen of which Ransome was at the helm. '*Lottie* proved herself a good little boat, though groaning and squeaking horribly during the worst of the battering.' When they finally brought her home to winter in Hillyard's yard, they had covered over 600 miles.

The 1955 season followed the same congenial pattern as the last. But the mishaps inseparable from cruising were much more difficult to cope with now that Arthur was over seventy and chronically unhealthy. That autumn, he wrote to Colonel Busk: 'It was a grand sail yesterday, fresh fair wind, exactly of the strength that *Lottie* likes best. With obvious torrents of rain here, there and everywhere all round, but sunshine for *Lottie*, easily the best sail of the year.' The letter also explained that they had decided to wind up and sell *Lottie*. 'Genia has long decided that we are to stop and I suppose we are a bit old . . . So now I swallow the anchor with one gulp and henceforth think exclusively in terms of fishing.' He was seventy-one that year and wrote a poem to mark the occasion.

> Seventy-one!
> It isn't much fun
> To be Seventy-one.
> Wool's nearly spun:
> Sand's nearly run:
> The end has begun:
> Life's nearly DONE.
> It isn't much fun
> To be Seventy-one.

In 1957, Ellen Tillinghast and family visited the Ransomes in Hurlingham Court, following up an invitation that Arthur had issued ten years earlier, when she wrote to praise *Great Northern?*. Let in by Evgenia, they immediately noticed a notice on a door saying 'Kitchen. Keep Out'. Ransome was 'a large, bright-eyed old man with a white moustache and white hair around a bald spot'. He wore an old pepper-and-salt tweed jacket over a grey sweater, dark trousers and black slippers.

While Evgenia took the twins and their sister Elizabeth upstairs, Ransome showed Ellen an old photograph of his great-grandfather, the Reverend John Jackson, and his grandmother, Hannah Jackson. On the wall were portraits of all the boats he had owned, including *Racundra*. In the dining room was a table groaning under an enormous tea – 'a large fruit cake, a three-tiered iced Madeira cake, a plateful of assorted biscuits, a piled plate of squares of buttered bread, a pot of honey, a dish of strawberry jam, and a tray with the tea service on it'. Ransome told the girls not to start with bread and butter, 'a dreadful custom which filled you up before you get to the more important things like cake'. The rum-butter icing on the cake was a Lakeland farm tradition, he said, and described the winter hound trails, after which the huntsmen downed mugs of hot rum with a large lump of butter stirred into it, and then sank to sleep under feather mattresses. Afterwards, the Ransomes got out photographs of Low Ludderburn and the Broads, and reminisced about all the young crews who had enlivened their voyages. When they left, Ransome chuckled benignly when the children threw their arms 'as far around his middle as they would go'.

RETREAT TO RUSLAND

And I have asked to be
Where no storms come,
Where the green swell is in the havens dumb,
And out of the swing of the sea.
Gerard Manley Hopkins, 'Heaven-Haven'

The Ransomes at last resolved their inability to choose between London and the north by renting a cottage in the Lakes but keeping their London flat. They bought a new car, a Wolseley 4/44 saloon, and on 3 May 1955, Ransome headed north in her, did some fishing in his old haunts, and found Earlinghearth Cottage, on the northern edge of Haverthwaite in the Rusland Valley, a secret place tucked in a fold of the fells just south of Windermere and Coniston. Haverthwaite was home to his favourite inn, the Hark to Melody, and had a station. It was theirs, furnished and with upstairs bathroom, mains water and electricity for £25 a month.

The Ransomes rented Hill Top, Haverthwaite, in 1956, and bought it outright in 1960

Standing in an acre of its own woodland, it looked west; a large bay in the south wall flooded the sitting room with light. Rusland Pool was a short walk away, and the Leven was twenty minutes. As well as fishing, Ransome revisited his favourite fishing writers for a National Book League booklet. *Fishing*, a miracle of distilled description of 'time-tested old books and recommended new ones', was published in August 1955.

Next year, they found another cottage in Haverthwaite. Hill Top was a few hundred yards uphill from Earlinghearth, and the cat they had entertained the year before came up to join them. It was more spacious than Earlinghearth, with a barn and an acre of ground. 'We are beginning to feel we have been here a long time,' Ransome wrote to Rupert Hart-Davis after only two months.

Genia is as usual overworking in the nettle-choked wilderness she means to turn into a garden. The gutters round the roofs have been mended, slates placed over a yawning hole in the roof of the barn, the rodent operative has got rid of a fearful plague of other rodents as operative as himself, the barn door has been so altered as to make it easy to get my chariot in, Great Spotted Woodpeckers are busy in the oak below my windows, we see buzzards daily . . . We badly need rain so the weather will probably be fine. It is glorious today except for fishermen. I

LEFT Ransome with Rupert Hart-Davis at Hill Top
RIGHT Evgenia and Ransome beside Hill Top's old-fashioned
iron range

forgave it because it did rain last night after I had planted eighteen pansy seedlings. But that drop has not raised the river a quarter of an inch. We want a good deluge to bring the salmon bouncing in.

Hill Top cottage had lovely views up the Rusland Valley. The name Rusland derived from Ralf, or Ranulf's land; that of Ransome from Ranulf's son. It is also appropriately evocative of Russia. Arthur thought the graveyard of its church the quietest place in the world, and resolved to be buried there, under a Corsican pine that he particularly admired, so that he could hear the wind in its needles. They went to services there and at Finsthwaite, where Arthur particularly enjoyed the sermons: the vicar was a fishing friend, Roland Peddar.

During 1958, Arthur put together a second book of fishing essays, *Mainly About Fishing*, which he dedicated to Peddar. It is an enlightening insight into how lively his literary hinterland still was. In an essay on historic diaries that either mentioned fishing or were devoted to it, he quotes with relish the first entry in his own favourite, one kept by a north country vicar from the age of twelve: 'Caught sixteen sticklebacks and a minnow (I ate the minnow).' Dorothy Wordsworth, Kilvert and Parson Woodforde all feature. Delightful too is an essay about fishing rods called 'The Travelling Companion'. 'A rod in the rack over your head is to have the fishing faculties on the alert. The landscape swaying past the window is not a meaningless phantasmagoria. The rivers are no sleeping beauties but awake and beckoning.'

In December 1958, two months before the publication of *Mainly About Fishing*, Ransome slipped on the icy steps of Cape's Bedford Square offices. He was effectively bedridden for the next seven months; then he went to a Pagham nursing home to convalesce. There was no trip north in 1959, but in 1960 they decided to buy Hill Top cottage outright, though they kept the

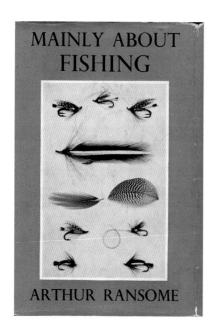

Hurlingham Court flat as a winter base until 1963. There was the usual upheaval as Evgenia summoned a new army of builders in order to get it the way she wanted it. Arthur's books were brought up from London in quantities. At the time of his death he had 250 biographies, over 400 books on sailing and navigation, 35 books on chess and over 300 on fishing, as well as a motley collection of fiction. These lined the shelves of his last real home as comfortingly as they had lined that of his first one, in Hatch.

Old friends were fading away. Barbara Gnosspelius died in 1961, Ernest in March 1962 and Ursula in July 1962. Arthur sent a touchingly affectionate letter of comfort to Dora. 'We linger on while all those younger ones have gone without waiting for us.' Barbara and Oscar's daughter Janet was a stalwart friend, constantly visiting from Liverpool and always ready to solve problems. Another asset was John Berry, then a young enthusiast for Arthur's books, who became an indefatigable helper with the garden and all kinds of odd jobs; his memories of the Ransomes at Hill Top are described in *Discovering Swallows and Amazons* (2004).

In 1963, Ransome went into hospital again, and was confined to a wheelchair on his return. His mind began to fade, but still occasionally sparkled into life. 'My dear Old Beetle,' he wrote to Dora in September. 'If only I could I should like to write you a good gossippy scrawl to remind you of sunsets seen from the old Lair at the bottom of the Lanehead garden. But I can't, and can only hope that you will understand and forgive me for being so incapable.' Dora died in 1964. In his eighties, Ransome become very frail in both body and mind. He was taken to the Cheadle Royal Hospital, near Manchester, in October 1965, and remained there until his death at the age of eighty-three on 3 June 1967. To have lived as long as he did with such an appalling record of health was a reflection of his unconquerable spirit. He was buried, as he wished, in Rusland churchyard. Evgenia moved south for the last eight years of her life, and was buried with him at Rusland in 1975.

SWALLOWS AND AMAZONS FOREVER

*'I believe that if these books about Swallows and Amazons live – and I cannot imagine
their not living a long time – it will be because they lay hold on the underlying continuity
of imaginative play, the heartfelt constructive make-believe that carries children
along from one generation to another.'*

Mary Lamberton-Becker, New York Herald Tribune, *1933*

Fifty years after Arthur Ransome died, all twelve of his books about the Swallows, the Amazons and the Ds are still in print in both paperback and hardback. They have been translated into many languages, including in recent years Japanese, Chinese, Czech and Estonian. A musical based on *Swallows and Amazons* was launched in 2010 and a new film version is under way. A room in the Museum of Lakeland Life & Industry in Kendal is devoted to memorabilia of Arthur Ransome given to the museum by his widow, Evgenia: his desk, his favourite chair, bookcases full of his books, and paintings and photographs of his family. Bank Ground Farm, scene of the genesis of *Swallows and Amazons* itself, now has a *Swallows and Amazons* Tea Room as well as holiday accommodation for those who want to sail in *Swallow*'s wake. A new venture, the Arthur Ransome Trust (www.arthur-ransome-trust.org.uk), is devoted to establishing a permanent Arthur Ransome centre in the Coniston area, so that pilgrims can

OPPOSITE Since they first appeared, Ransome's twelve books featuring the Swallows, the Amazons and the Ds have been much translated: this collage was made by Robert Thompson, a keen collector of the foreign editions

RIGHT Cover of the 2012 Vintage paperback of *Swallows and Amazons*

Abbot Hall, Kendal, has a fine display of Ransome memorabilia, including the desk that was once his father's, and many of his favourite books and photographs

be directed towards the many places he knew and loved. It runs events and exhibitions, and provides much interesting in-depth information about Ransome.

There have been several biographical works. Ransome's own very entertaining *Autobiography*, edited by Rupert Hart-Davis, was published after his death in 1976. Hugh Brogan's *Life of Arthur Ransome* (1984) is still illuminating. Roland Chambers' *The Last Englishman* (2009) is an eye-opening account of his years in Russia, which ends as he settles at his typewriter to begin *Swallows and Amazons*. My own *Arthur Ransome and Captain Flint's Trunk* (1984, updated 2007) is a hunt for the truth behind the stories made at a time when many of the people who contributed to them were still alive; researching it was a quest made the more entertaining by having my own four children in tow for much of it. Since then numerous books, most notably those of Roger Wardale and Ted Alexander, have made exciting discoveries about different aspects of Ransome's life and work.

The Arthur Ransome Society (TARS) (www.arthur-ransome.org) was founded at a celebration for the preservation of the dinghy Ransome immortalized as *Amazon*. Dedicated to furthering knowledge of Arthur Ransome, and providing opportunities for young people to enjoy sailing and camping, it has thriving branches all over the world as well as in Great Britain. Its publications have enormously deepened appreciation of Ransome's literary skill, and of every aspect of his interests, including bird-watching, chess and fishing. Every year, people gather from all over the world to enjoy its annual gathering, and every two years it holds a literary weekend, which never fails to offer new items of interest.

What of Arthur Ransome's boats? *Nancy Blackett* was saved from steady deterioration by Peter Willis, who established the Nancy Blackett Trust (www.nancyblackett.org), now a thriving body of enthusiasts who arrange passages in her to Holland and France. *Peter Duck* and the original *Lottie Blossom*, both owned by members of TARS, are active on the east coast. Three of the dinghies survive. *Amazon* can be seen at the Ruskin Museum, Coniston. Ransome's fishing dinghy *Coch-y-Bonddhu*, which became *Scarab* in *The Picts and The Martyrs,* has been acquired and restored by TARS; she is now in the care of Paul Flint at Windermere School. The original *Swallow* has disappeared without trace, but the *Swallow* that was tender to *Selina King* is now owned by Roger Wardale. Most recently the dinghy used as *Swallow* in the 1974 film has been restored by Magnus Smith and Robert Boden, thanks to generous donations from lovers of Ransome's books. Like *Nancy Blackett*, she now appears at a variety of events around the country and is made available for enthusiasts to sail (see www.sailransome.org), and so to experience adventure in true Ransome style.

ABOVE Titty with *Amazon*, from the 1974 film directed by Claude Waltham

BELOW The Hampshire family sailing in the dinghy used as *Swallow* in the 1974 film and now restored by Magnus Smith

FURTHER READING

Brogan, Hugh, *The Life of Arthur Ransome*, Cape, 1984: the first, and still the best, all-round biography of Ransome

—, *Signalling From Mars: The Letters of Arthur Ransome*, Cape, 1997

Chambers, Roland, *The Last Englishman*, Faber, 2009: focuses on Ransome in Russia

Findlay, Kirsty Nichol, *Arthur Ransome's Long-lost Study of Robert Louis Stevenson*, Boydell & Brewer, 2011: sheds new light on Ransome as a literary critic

Hammond, Wayne, *Arthur Ransome: A Bibliography*, Oak Knoll Press, 2000: an incredibly useful and comprehensive guide to Ransome's books and articles, and to later publications about him

Hardyment, Christina, *Arthur Ransome and Captain Flint's Trunk*, Frances Lincoln, 2007

Ransome, Arthur, *Autobiography*, Cape, 1976

—, *Racundra's First Cruise*, edited by Brian Hammett, Fernhurst, 2002

—, and Hammett, Brian, *Racundra's Third Cruise*, Fernhurst, 2003: compiled by Hammett from Ransome's sailing logs and notebooks, this also contains the interrupted second cruise

Townend, Matthew, *The Vikings and Victorian Lakeland: The Norse Medievalism of W.G. Collingwood and his Contemporaries*, Cumberland and Westmorland Antiquarian and Archaeological Society, 2009

Wardale, Roger, *Arthur Ransome, Master Story-Teller*, Great Northern, 2010

—, *Arthur Ransome Under Sail*, Sigma, 2010

Books privately published for members of the Arthur Ransome Society (TARS)

Andrews, Judy, *Arthur Ransome's Family 1649–1975*, 2002

Alexander, Ted, with an additional essay by Margaret Ratcliffe, *Ransome At Home*, Amazon Publications, 1996

Alexander, Ted, and Verizhnikova, Tatiana, *Ransome in Russia*, Amazon Publications, 2003

Cowen, John, *A Ransome Bookcase*, Amazon Publications, 2000

Sewart, Dave, *Illustrating Arthur Ransome*, Amazon Publications, 1994

Thompson, Robert, *Arthur Ransome's Foreign Legion*, Amazon Publications, 2009

The TARS journal, *Mixed Moss*, and its *Literary Transactions*, the record of papers given at the biennial Literary Weekend, stretch back twenty years; they are both treasure troves of research into Ransome's life and writings.

The TARS library is an exceptionally broad-reaching collection of books connected with Arthur Ransome, including many interesting original research papers.

The Brotherton Library at the University of Leeds and the Abbot Hall Art Gallery and Lakeland Museum in Kendal all hold excellent collections relating to Ransome's life and writings.

INDEX

Page numbers in *italics* refer captions to the illustrations;
the abbreviation 'AR' refers to Arthur Ransome

ACKNOWLEDGMENTS

AUTHOR'S ACKNOWLEDGMENTS

First and foremost I must thank Roger Wardale and Ted Alexander for their generous help with proofreading and the sourcing of photographs, as well as their invaluable published studies of different aspects of Arthur Ransome. My fellow executors of the Arthur Ransome Literary Estate, Geraint Lewis and Elizabeth Sewart, have contributed in many ways, as have John Cowen, an expert in early Ransome editions, Jeremy Gibson, one of the first and hardest-working members of the Arthur Ransome Society, and David Hambledon, Secretary of the Trojan Trust. Margaret Ratcliffe, founder of the Arthur Ransome Society's imaginatively conceived and extensive library, has been generous with her time and knowledge of Ransome in Paris. I am grateful too for Judy Andrews' research into Ransome's ancestors, and for the hospitality which she and her husband Jim afforded me.

I am very grateful indeed for the quick and efficient help and facilities for research given by Chris Sheppard, Cindy Tsegmid and the staff of the Brotherton Library in Leeds, and James Arnold and the staff of the Abbot Hall Art Gallery and Lakeland Museum in Kendal, the main repositories of Arthur Ransome's archives. Robert Thompson lent me SD *Hirondelle* to explore Coniston Water afresh, and Paul and Caroline Johnson responded with magnificent generosity to an act of piracy on inland waters by sailing with me in SD *Arbeia* to Wild Cat Island, on a day perfectly suited to photography.

Peter Willis, prime mover of the Nancy Blackett Trust, Ted Evans, owner of *Ragged Robin* (formerly *Lottie Blossom*), and Julia Jones, owner of *Peter Duck*, all helped with information and photographs.

Paul and Cecilia Flint provided not just a roof over my head but warm hospitality when I visited Windermere, where they are bringing up their family in the true spirit of Arthur Ransome, and this book is dedicated to them.

PICTURE CREDITS

The author and publisher thank the following copyright owners for permission to reproduce their illustrations on the pages listed after their names. Every effort has been made to provide correct attributions. Any inadvertent errors or omissions will be corrected in subsequent editions of this book.

a=above b=below c =centre l=left r=right

Arthur Ransome Literary Estate 1, 3, 5, 8, 10, 12, 13a, 13b, 16, 21l, 22l, 22r, 29, 31, 32, 36al, 36ar, 38, 39r, 40, 41, 44a, 44b, 45, 46, 48, 49, 51l, 52, 53l, 53r, 54r, 57, 58l, 58r, 59a, 59b, 60, 61, 62, 63, 64, 65l, 65r, 66a, 66b, 67, 68, 70, 71l, 73r, 76, 77l, 77r, 78, 79, 80, 81al, 81ar, 81bl, 82r, 83a, 83b, 84, 87, 89a, 89b, 90, 91a, 91bl, 92, 93, 94r, 97r, 98, 99r, 102l and r, 103al, 103ar, 103b, 105l, 107, 108, 109b, 110, 111, 113, 114, 116, 117, 118, 119l, 121, 128l, 128r, 132, 133, 136l, 136r, 139l, 139r, 140, 141, 145l, 145r, 148l, 148r, 149l, 160
Arthur Ransome Literary Estate/Jonathan Cape 81br, 82l, 91br, 95, 99l, 106, 115, 121b, 129r, 131r, 151
Author's collection 4, 15a, 17, 18, 27a, 51r, 71r, 73l, 85
Ted Alexander 21r, 23, 24l, 30, 42, 56, 109a, 144, 147
Helen Caldwell 70r
Collingwood family 26r, 28, 35, 36b, 37a, 75l, 75r

Fiona Gilroy 6
Hawkshead benefice 149r
Julia Jones 137
Museum of Lakeland Life & Industry/reproduced by courtesy of Abbot Hall Art Gallery, Kendal, Cumbria 152
Dick Kelsall 74
National Trust Archive 126
Private collection 142–3
Queens Club Gardens Residents Association 37b
U.A. Ryaskov 55
NRM/Science and Society Picture Library 100
www.jon-sparks.co.uk 2, 72, 86, 87, 124
Uig Lodge 134
Magnus Smith 153
Courtesy of Studiocanal Films Ltd 153
Robert Thompson 150 and author photo on back flap
Vintage Classics 151
Roger Wardale 97l, 105r, 112, 119r, 131l

Reproduction of ARLE images in their care is by courtesy of the Brotherton Library, University of Leeds and Abbot Hall Art Gallery, Kendal, Cumbria. The author is also grateful for the assistance of Ted Alexander, the Colwell Collection, the Garrick Club, David Hambledon, Robert Thompson, Roger Wardale and private sources in whose collections other pictures used in this book are located.

Ransome's tailpiece from *Swallows and Amazons*

TEXT ACKNOWLEDGMENTS

Copyright in all quotations lies with the Arthur Ransome Literary Estate, except for a short passage from Dora Collingwood's diary, which rests with the Altounyan family.